Equal Or Greater Force

Developing the Proper Mindset in Order to Confront and Survive a Violent Criminal or Terrorist Act

by

Kit Cessna

authorHOUSE

1663 LIBERTY DRIVE, SUITE 200
BLOOMINGTON, INDIANA 47403
(800) 839-8640
WWW.AUTHORHOUSE.COM

This book is a work of non-fiction. Names of people and places have been changed to protect their privacy.

© 2005 Kit Cessna
All Rights Reserved.

No part of this book may be reproduced, stored in a retrieval system, or transmitted by any means without the written permission of the author.

First published by AuthorHouse 12/30/04

ISBN: 1-4208-0969-5 (e)
ISBN: 1-4208-0968-7(sc)

Library of Congress Control Number: 2004098555

Printed in the United States of America
Bloomington, Indiana

This book is printed on acid-free paper.

Acknowledgements

Writing this book was a journey into the unknown. Though my friends have encouraged me to undertake a book project for many years, I only recently decided to give it a try. To the following individuals and institutions I give my thanks.

My beautiful wife, Stephanie, for pushing me to continue the work despite all the distractions and pressures that life has thrown at us, and for reminding me that the English language does have rules, and one is required to follow them.

Sheriff Jeff Wiley of the Ascension Parish Sheriff's Office and Chief Greg Phares (retired) of the Baton Rouge Police Department, for facilitating my entry into the world of law enforcement.

Lieutenant Tommy Rice of the East Baton Rouge Sheriff's Office for his insights into the procedures followed in the investigation of a self-defense shooting, and Attorneys Floyd Falcon and Leuanne Greco of Baton Rouge, for their insights into the legal aftermath of a self-defense shooting.

Last, but definitely not least, the United States Army for giving me the experience and background necessary to write this book.

Dedication

This book is dedicated to the memories of the following people:

- Master Sergeant Gary Gordon and Sergeant First Class Randy Shugart, United States Army Delta Force. Both were killed in action in Mogadishu, Somalia, in 1993 and were posthumously awarded the Medal of Honor. In a doomed attempt to rescue their downed comrades, these two American soldiers unhesitatingly threw themselves into a situation that they knew they could not survive. I knew them both, and the memory of their faces, friendship, and laughter will be with me all my days.

- The passengers of United Airlines flight 93 who attacked the terrorists in an attempt to recapture the hijacked aircraft. In their last few moments, these valiant souls decided to go down fighting and their bravery saved thousands of their fellow citizens and quite possibly the very existence of our government.

I hope all of you have had a chance to meet in the afterlife, for you are kindred spirits.

Table of Contents

Acknowledgements v

Dedication vii

Introduction xi

Chapter 1 The Casualties 1

Chapter 2 Why do these things happen? 12

Chapter 3 Life and liberty; the gift from long ago 25

Chapter 4 Developing a stay-alive mindset 43

Chapter 5 How to have a fight; facing the actual confrontation; .. 60

Chapter 6 The weapons in the arsenal 88

Chapter 7 The Aftermath 111

Epilogue 125

Introduction

This book, being philosophical in nature, deals primarily with the attitude and mindset necessary to have a chance to survive a violent attack on yourself or your loved ones. This is not a pleasant subject, but in this violent world, a necessary one. The possibility of finding yourself in a life-threatening situation is something that you must consider in order to maintain a realistic outlook on life.

My target audience is the average citizen of all ages and backgrounds who has not had any formal training or experience in the subject of staying alive in a lethal confrontation with another human being. Because this is the type of person that I am reaching out to, I have had to think long and hard about what I say and how I was going to say it. I don't want to make this subject any more grim than necessary, but at the same time I don't want to sugar coat it in any manner. I believe that I managed to hit a happy medium, but you will be the judge of that.

This work consists of a close examination of a number of different subjects that all work toward a central theme. In the first chapter are descriptions of four brutal crimes that were committed against average American citizens. I don't give any names or identities to the victims or the towns that they live in. While all of these incidents actually happened in a specific time and place to real people, I want you to view them as something that could happen to you. The second chapter is a hard look at where we are today when it comes to the mindset of the average citizen in facing a lethal threat. We have lost a lot of ground in this area and we need to gain some of that ground back.

The third chapter takes you through a close look at the rest of the world and makes some stark comparisons between them and us. Things are not always as they seem, and the rest of the world is still very different than we are in many respects. The purpose of the chapter is to point out those differences and to make you appreciate the freedoms that we have and will hopefully continue to have. In chapter four, I will describe the mindset necessary to have a chance of survival in the event of a violent attack. Developing a mindset is the first step toward competent self-defense, so read it carefully.

Chapter five contains specific advice on how to think and what to do during an actual encounter. This will not be a pleasant chapter for some, but it is the most important one in the book in many ways. While this book was not written to be a self-defense manual, chapter six will cover the weapons available to the average citizen and will explain the advantages and disadvantages of each one. The final chapter is an explanation of the events that will happen in the aftermath of a defensive use of lethal force by a private citizen.

All of the opinions offered in this book are mine and mine alone. They represent the conclusions that I have come to during twenty-five years of dealing with this subject. I make no apology for them and will stand by them, though I know that not all of you will agree with what I have had to say. That is fine; the ability to disagree with each other is one of the great things about life in this nation. However, if you do find yourself in disagreement with my ideas, I would ask two things of you. First, read on and make your final judgment after you have completed this book. Second, look in the mirror and come up with some solutions or ideas that are superior to mine. Be honest with yourself as you do this and remember the grim circumstances that we are talking about. When you do come up with your answers, ask yourself if you are willing to bet your life on them.

Thank you for reading and I hope you enjoy the book.

Chapter 1
The Casualties

"Society needs to condemn a little more and understand a little less".

John Major

A light afternoon rain is falling as an attractive, middle aged woman turns into her driveway. Her home is located in a typical upper-middle-class neighborhood, each yard trimmed and landscaped. Pulling up to the garage door, she pushes the button on the remote control and waits as it rumbles upward. As she waits, she looks at her house and thinks about how safe she feels living in this neighborhood. When the door is finished ascending, she slowly guides the vehicle through the opening. She is glad to be home; since the kids had left for school that morning she has been rushing all over town trying to complete the week's errands. She is so focused on other matters that she fails to notice a dark blue van turning onto the street behind her. Once inside the garage, the woman turns the vehicle off and gets out. Looking at the piles of groceries on the back seat, she tries to calculate how long it will take her to put them all away. In less than thirty minutes a school bus will come to a stop a few houses down, unloading a mass of noisy children. Among this group of youngsters will be three of her own. She thinks to herself, "If I hurry and get all the groceries put away, there will still be time for a nice hot, relaxing bath." Opening the back door of her car, she grabs several bags of food and moves to the kitchen door, fumbling with her keys. As she struggles with the bags and the doorknob, she again fails to notice the van that has now stopped across the street.

Inside the van, the man listens to the intermittent squeak of the windshield wipers as they flick the water off the glass in front of him. Chewing on a toothpick, he watches the woman inside the garage, seeing her move from the kitchen door, to the car, and back again. Catching his own reflection in the rear view mirror, he studies himself for a moment, and then looks back across the street. His outward calmness belies the excitement that he feels as he watches his victim. She had caught his eye a couple of hours ago as she exited her sport utility vehicle in the grocery store parking lot. Maneuvering into a parking space a few yards down from hers, he patiently waited for her to come back out. When she finally reappeared, pushing a heavily laden cart, he stared at her through the tinted glass, trying to make up his mind.

A man of specific tastes and desires, he had contemplated her movements as she loaded the back seat. "A little on the tall side and probably dyes her hair," he mused. She doesn't really fit the profile that he is looking for, but he continues to observe anyway. It has been months since the last one and he feels the need for action. Finished with the loading, the woman had pushed her cart in front of her car and entered the vehicle. As she backed out, the man had decided to follow her. Staying a few vehicles back, he had trailed her through the steadily building afternoon traffic. Several times during the ride the man almost decided to let her go, but something made him stay behind her. It was when she turned through the gate into her subdivision that he had finally made up his mind.

Inside the house the woman moves quickly back and forth across the kitchen, taking items out of the bags and putting them away. As she works, she can hear the gurgle and splash of the bathwater running and she anticipates relaxing in its soapy warmth. The sound of the running water covers the sound of the van as it backs up the driveway and comes to a stop behind her own vehicle. In her haste, the woman has left the garage and kitchen door open. Finishing with the groceries, she walks across the kitchen and turns down the hall. As she passes the kitchen door, she doesn't see the man standing in the garage staring at her. Moving back to her bedroom the woman begins to undress for her bath. Looking at the clock on the dresser, she realizes that she has only fifteen minutes before her children are due to get off the bus. "Plenty of time," she thinks, "They will spend another ten minutes talking to their friends before they come to the house". Naked, she turns toward the hallway and comes face to face with the man.

The shock and fear that slam into her system are so overpowering that she cannot even scream. For a couple of seconds she stares, bug eyed at the intruder who grins back at her. "Yeah, you will do just fine bitch," he says. "You will be just what I need." Still grinning, he begins to move toward her. The woman sucks in her breath for the beginning of a scream, but the man is far too fast. His right fist lashes out, catching her on the side of the face and driving her head into the doorframe behind her. There is a bright flash in her vision and she hears herself thump onto the bedroom floor. As her consciousness fades, there is blackness.

Moving quickly, the man takes a look out the front window to see if his presence at the house has been noticed. Satisfied that is has not, he shoves the living room furniture to the side, uncovering a large rug in the middle of the room. Returning to the bedroom, he grabs the woman by the feet and pulls her down the hall and through the kitchen. In the living room he rolls her onto the edge of the rug and then rolls her up in it. She is taller than he had thought and therefore heavier. It takes him ten minutes to drag the bundle back through the kitchen and out into the garage. Another few minutes are required for him to lift the rug-wrapped body up into the van. Once inside the van, he wraps the bundle in rope, tying a series of knots along its length, effectively binding the woman inside it.

Finished at last, he returns to the kitchen and pulls the refrigerator door open. Scanning through the contents, he selects a bottle of mineral water and puts it in his side pocket. Returning to the garage, he again scans the neighborhood for a sign that others have been alerted to his presence. Seeing no danger, he gets into the van and pulls slowly down the driveway. Looking left and right and still sensing no threat, he drives toward the entrance of the neighborhood. As he drives out, the school bus drives in.

Three months later the woman's remains are discovered on the edge of a marshy area on the outskirts of town. There is little left as the effects of decomposition and the attentions of wild animals have taken their toll. Visual identification is impossible, and her identity is unknown for several days. Finally, a DNA match is made and her family is informed of her fate.

On the day that the woman's body is discovered, in another town, in another state, a twenty-year-old college sophomore starts the day with a pre-dawn jog. The fall air is cold and crisp as it blows across the lakes surrounding the local university and the horizon is beginning to lighten in the east. After the brutal heat of the summer, the coolness feels delicious as it passes over her face. It is her favorite time of year, and she cannot resist an early morning run despite the repeated warnings that a serial killer may be working the area. She is aware that at least one girl her age is missing but she doesn't know the details and has made no effort to find out. As the miles pass, she revels in the sensations of a strong body, her breath coming steadily and easily. Rounding the lake and moving back toward her dormitory, she comes to a part of the route that passes through a vacant lot. On the other side of the lot, where the running trail again meets the street, sits an aging pick-up truck. Concentrating on her run, she doesn't notice that the vehicle's engine is running, the white exhaust floating in the air behind it. Nor does she see the man sitting in the cab watching her approach. As she comes closer, the man reaches over and opens his door a crack.

Although he has positioned his vehicle in front of her path, the man has actually followed the girl for most of her run. Sighting her as she left her dormitory, he had hung back and remained out of her view until he confirmed that she was taking her usual route. He had followed her several times over the weeks and had become familiar with her movements. Once he had verified that she was on her regular course, he had taken a shortcut and positioned his truck on the other side of the vacant lot ahead of her.

The Casualties

As the girl comes around the front of the truck to continue down the street, the man grabs the door with both hands and slams it directly into her face. He outweighs her by at least one hundred pounds and the force of his blow stops her forward momentum and throws her back. Stunned by the blow, she falls on her back in the street, holding her hands to her mouth. Several of her front teeth have been broken off by the impact and her mouth is filling with blood. As she chokes and spits, she is still unaware of what has actually happened and therefore doesn't even see the man run toward her. Reaching her, he kicks her in the head, knocking her flat onto the ground.

He is out in the open and, even though it is not yet light, he is taking a considerable risk and works fast. Pulling a heavy plastic strap out of his jacket pocket, he grabs her hands and wrenches them around behind her. He then loops the strap over her wrists and yanks it tight. Digging in his other pocket, he comes out with a small roll of silver duct tape. Grabbing her hair, he jerks her to a sitting position and wraps the tape around her head and mouth, gagging her. Still holding her by the hair, he pulls her to her feet and forces her toward the truck. Once there, he pushes her into the passenger side of the cab and onto the floor. Looking around, he puts the truck in gear and pulls away from the lot. On the floor the girl begins to whimper and moan. The man takes his foot off the accelerator and kicks her several times, silencing her.

The girl's body is never found. For years after her disappearance, her mother breaks down sobbing on her birthday.

On the same day that the girl disappeared, in yet another town, a young cashier stares through the windows of a convenience store as darkness falls. Looking around the empty store, he sighs with boredom. "Not much of a job", he thinks, "but it will do until something better comes along." Struggling through his first year of college, he works here because he can be employed fulltime and still go to classes. Since he is paying his own way through school, a steady source of income is important. The store is located in a crime-ridden area, and his family doesn't like him working there, but he insists that he can handle it. Like most young men in his age group, he has never been confronted with real violence and maintains a naïve and trusting attitude towards the world around him. He has a totally unrealistic belief in his own immortality and the good will of his fellow man. That perspective will soon change.

Moving back behind the counter, he pays scant attention to the battered gray sedan backing into a parking slot directly in front of the doors. Three men occupy the vehicle and as the driver stays behind the wheel, the other two get out and scan the surrounding area. Satisfied, they walk into the store and look around. One of the men proceeds to the rear and pretends to be looking at the racks of bottles behind the frosted glass. The other man moves to a side aisle, out of sight of the cashier. Making eye contact with each other, they nod and start toward the counter. The young man sees them coming and politely asks if he can help them with something. Their response stuns him.

Yanking a small automatic pistol out of his jacket pocket, the taller of the two men thrusts the gun in the cashier's face and snarls, "You bet yo ass you can help us, mutherfucker! Git yo narrow little ass in that drawer and git that money out here, bitch!". Taken totally by surprise, the young man can only stare at the robber. Taking his lack of response as non-compliance, the man reaches across the counter and smashes the pistol barrel into the cashier's face. The young man is knocked backward into a shelf and falls to the floor in a cascade of cigarette cartons. Blood gushes out of his broken nose and splatters on his shirt. Never having been in a situation like this, the cashier stares up at his attacker with disbelief. "Git the fuck up off that floor and git the money, mutherfucker! I ain't goin a tell you again! Next time I'll shoot yo college boy ass!". The robber's eyes are full of pure hatred as the terrified cashier struggles to his feet. In this moment of fear and stress, all the young man can think of is to do what he has always been told to do when confronted with a violent criminal. He will give the man what he says he wants and everything should be okay. Opening the cash drawer, he scoops all the money out onto the counter and steps back, hand to his nose. The second robber begins rapidly counting the bills, stuffing them into a small paper bag. There is not much money to count and he finishes quickly, muttering a figure to his partner.

"Forty three dollars?, the man explodes, "Forty three mutherfuckin dollars, you little cunt? You think I'm going to walk out of here with that little bit of shit?" "You git the rest or I'm goin a kill yo ass right here, bitch!" The terrified young man tries to explain that that is all the money he has access to. Like most stores of that type, the money is put through a slot into a safe as it is collected and very little is left in the control of the cashier. The robber doesn't believe him and continues his barrages of threats, waving the pistol in the young man's face.

Getting nervous, the second robber tells his partner that it is time to go. "We been here too long man, lets git!" His partner stares at him for a moment and then nods. As they both walk toward the front door, the cashier's heart is thundering in his chest. He is hurt and badly shaken but, at this moment, he thinks that it is over. He could not be more wrong. Reaching the door, the second robber moves outside and goes directly to the car. His partner starts outside and then stops. Looking back at the shaking cashier, the expression on his face changes from anger to pure malevolence. Without saying a word, he walks over to the young man, raises the pistol, and shoots him in the face. The sound of the shot reverberates through the small store as the young man falls. The robber looks at the still body and the spreading pool of blood, shrugs, and walks out of the store. A few seconds later, the sound of squealing tires is heard from the parking lot.

The young man is not dead, but he is near to it. The bullet has struck him in the mouth, smashing his lower jaw. A small sliver of jawbone has been driven through the back of his neck and into his spinal column. He will never regain consciousness.

Eighteen months after the shooting, with all hope exhausted, the young man's family gathers at his bedside to say goodbye. One by one they stroke his hair and tell him that they love him. His mother tells him to take care of himself when he gets to heaven. There is no response other than the hiss of the artificial life support system. After a long moment, the young man's father nods at the physician and the hissing stops.

A few weeks after the young man dies, it is the beginning of a busy day at a major airport. Thousands of early morning travelers are moving through the ticketing and check-in process. Dozens of aircraft are parked at the gates as an army of maintenance personnel and luggage handlers swarm around them. Long lines of passengers shuffle through the security checkpoint as the loudspeakers blare in the background. Conveyor belts hum, pulling small carry-on bags through the x-ray tunnel while bored security officers watch the screens. The magnetic detector beeps occasionally, resulting in a few people being subjected to further scrutiny. Despite these short delays, the bulk of the passengers are soon moving out to the departure gates, awaiting the signal to board. Most of the flights are full and when the announcement is given to begin boarding, there is a steady movement of humanity down the jet way and into the aircraft. People move down the aisles, identifying their seats and shoving their bags into the luggage racks above them. Snatches of conversation are only interrupted by the sound of small doors slamming as the racks are filled and closed.

It is an international airport, a gateway for people from all over the planet, and nobody pays any particular attention to the nationality of those around them. The four young men of Middle Eastern descent draw hardly a glance as they calmly settle into their seats. As the aircraft backs away from the gate, the flight attendant gives the safety briefing over the loudspeaker. While few of the passengers actually listen to the briefing, these four watch her closely. A few minutes later, the aircraft is hurtling down the concrete runway with a roar. Breaking free of the ground, it begins a smooth climb into the cold morning air.

Twenty minutes later the aircraft is gliding through the clouds toward its final cruising altitude on its way to a West Coast destination.

Inside, the passengers are settling down for a routine flight. A few travelers push their seats back and close their eyes, hoping to sleep through the five-hour trip. Some busy themselves with books and magazines or engage others in conversation. The flight attendants move toward the galley to begin the process of serving drinks and snacks. For a short time all is calm and routine and then that time ends.

Without warning, two of the Middle Eastern males rise from their seats and move directly toward the cockpit. Hands in their pockets, they move quickly and decisively. As they pass through the forward galley, one of the two flight attendants at that location turns, a quizzical look on her face, and asks if she can help them. They both stop and stare at her for a minute while she repeats the question. One of the men calmly pulls a razor knife out of his pocket and snaps the blade open. Staring at the flight attendant with eyes completely devoid of emotion, he steps toward her and slashes her across the face. Staggering back, she instinctively raises her hand to her face as a cascade of blood spatters the front of her white shirt. Sinking to the floor, she begins to scream.

The other flight attendant stares in shock as the hijacker steps across the body of his first victim and slashes her across the chest. She screams and tries to turn away and as she does, he slashes her again and again across the back. Soon she is crumpled on the floor with her co-worker. The women's screams have caught the attention of most of the passengers, and this noise has also served to galvanize two other hijackers into action. Fishing into their pockets and pulling out their own razor knives, they launch a frenzied attack on the rest of the passengers. The purpose of the assault is intimidation, and they move rapidly down the aisles screaming, shoving, and slashing. Here and there the razors find their mark and soon the walls of the passenger compartment are sprinkled with blood. After a few minutes of pandemonium, the two hijackers have the entire compartment under control.

In the front galley, one of the hijackers reaches over to the flight attendant who had been cut in the face and yanks her roughly to her feet. He turns her toward the cockpit door and slams her into it. "Yes, you will open this door. You will open it now!" the man screams in heavily accented English. "You will open this door now or I will kill this woman!" Inside the cockpit the Captain and first officer look at each other in disbelief. They have both had to deal with unruly passengers in the past, but neither has experienced anything like this. To have their passengers and crewmembers so savagely attacked is something that has never happened before.

Getting no response from the cockpit, the hijacker slashes the flight attendant across her back, causing her to shriek in pain. Slamming her back against the door, he repeats his demand. "You will open the door or I will kill this woman!" he shouts. With the life of one of their people in severe danger; the men in the cockpit decide to give in. The first officer moves to the door and unlocks it. He has no sooner finished turning the bolt when the door bursts inward and the hijacker forces his way into the cockpit. Waving his bloody razor in the first officer's face, he screams at him to get out. As he moves to comply, the first officer is thinking what he has been trained to think his entire adult life. "If we stay calm and give these maniacs what they want, everything will be okay." Surprising all of the occupants of the cockpit, the other hijacker leans over to the Captain and demands that he vacate his seat. "You want what? the Captain asks. "Yes you will move from your seat. I am in command of this aircraft now," the hijacker states. "So, who is going to fly this thing, buddy?" the Captain queries. "I will fly this aircraft you infidel pig, now get out of your seat," the hijacker retorts. For a moment the pilot is tempted to give in to the demand. Something deep inside him, however, tells him not to. He looks up at the hijacker with defiance and refuses. His resistance does no good. Without hesitation, the hijacker grabs the captain by the hair and forces his head back, exposing his throat, and slashes several times with the razor. Outside the cockpit the first officer is suffering the same fate and his body joins those of the two flight attendants, lying in a spreading pool of blood.

The Casualties

    The two hijackers in the front now occupy the cockpit. One of them sits in the captain's seat and scans the multitude of instruments in front of him, seemingly understanding what he sees. He then turns to the other hijacker and gives him a nod. This hijacker moves back into the passenger compartment clutching his bloody razor. He is splattered with blood from head to toe and presents a horrifying sight to the travelers. "Listen to me," he shouts, "Listen to me all people," "We are in command of this aircraft. There is a bomb aboard and we are returning to the airport." Continuing down the aisle, he gives more orders. "You will all remain calm in your seats," he states, "and you will make us no trouble." As the realization of what has happened settles in among the passengers, most of them are thinking similar thoughts. "If we just stay calm and give them what they want, we will be okay," is the common idea. Trained from birth to surrender in the face of a violent criminal attack, they huddle in their seats offering no resistance to the hijackers. Even though they outnumber their attacker by over thirty-to-one, they will remain this way for the rest of the flight.

    After a few moments, the aircraft begins making a slow and steady turn to the left until it is flying in the opposite direction. Thirty-five minutes later, traveling at almost five hundred miles an hour, it slams into a huge skyscraper. All aboard are consumed in the fireball.

Chapter 2
Why do these things happen?

"This incident does much to prove that America is nothing but a paper tiger ready to run away at the first sign of death or difficulty."

Osama Bin Laden (speaking about the pullout of U.S. forces from Somalia in 1993)

The incidents described in the first chapter did not come from my imagination. They are all based upon actual occurrences. We hear or read about incidents like these almost every single day and the place where I live is no different. In the summer of 2002, the citizens of Baton Rouge, Louisiana, were shocked to discover that they had a serial killer lurking among them. During the previous ten years, the city had suffered over 29 unsolved homicides of women. The three latest murders had just been linked by DNA evidence to the same killer. The killings were extremely brutal and, like other cities that have gone through this ordeal, Baton Rouge was gripped by fear and uncertainty. Suddenly the streets of this small southern city perched on the east bank of the Mississippi River didn't seem as friendly as they once were.

In September of the previous year, the citizens of Baton Rouge and the rest of the nation, were witness to one of the most brutal mass murders in the history of humanity. Thousands of innocent people were incinerated, vaporized, or crushed out of existence under tons of falling debris in what was left of the World Trade Center. Hundreds more were burned to death or buried under the rubble of the Pentagon. Suddenly, the United States of America was a different place and would never be the same again.

Why do these things happen?

Living in a world where the threat of deadly physical attack is more of a reality than ever before, many of us are asking a logical question. How did things come to be this way, and how long will this go on? Why are local criminals and foreign terrorists so bent on our personal destruction? The answers to these questions are not pleasant but they are simple.

They attack us because they know that they can

In the minds of both the international terrorist and the local violent criminal, we are a society of cowards. On the international front, the terrorist organizations in this world know that we possess the ability to project military force at a level that is unprecedented in human history. If we choose to use that force, no nation or organization can stand against us for long. They also know that as a nation we seem to have little stomach for a prolonged fight. We may win a quick initial victory but if the situation drags on for any length of time, we will seek reasons to run. Kill some of our soldiers or blow up a few buildings, and we will put our tail between our legs and slink away. The terrorists know this about us because that is exactly what we have done time and time again. If you don't believe me, just look at our recent history.

Our retreat from the world scene started in the early 1950's with the end of the Korean War, when we lacked the resolve to destroy the communist threat in that part of the world once and for all despite having more than enough military power to do so. Everyone called it an armistice, but it was a retreat and the whole world knew it. Following the Korean conflict, we stumbled through the twelve years of the Vietnam War without any clear direction or resolve and at the same time never lost a single major engagement to the enemy. In 1972 we whimpered and crawled away despite the fact that we had literally blown our opponent's military structure out of existence. So badly did we savage the Viet Cong and the North Vietnamese Army that after we withdrew in 1972, it took them three long years to rebuild to the point that they could overwhelm the south in 1975.

In the years following the Vietnam conflict, our track record did not get any better. The next conflict that we became involved in was the situation following the Israeli invasion of Lebanon in 1982. Again, we went into a situation with no clear direction, passion, or willpower. Late in 1983, a local terrorist group launched a suicide bomber attack, killing over 200 U.S. Marines. Despite the fact that the very same week we had just won a dramatic victory over communist expansion in Grenada, we again pulled our people out and slunk home in defeat. In 1989, we invaded Panama in order to destroy the brutal regime of Manuel Noriega. The victory was swift and there was no real aftermath to the operation. Panama quickly returned to normal, so this became one of the few times that we did not run. I maintain, however, that Panama could have gone either way, and if it had turned ugly, we would have fled the scene eventually.

Late in 1989 and early 1990 came the first Gulf War. Once again, we were initially victorious and, once again, we lacked the determination and fortitude to see the thing through to the actual end. Shortly after the end of hostilities, we left, running out on our allies, leaving a monster in power, and condemning others to have to deal with him again fourteen years later.

In late 1993 came our most flagrant act of national cowardice. U.S. troops had been sent to Somalia the year before to attempt to bring some stability to that country and to ensure the delivery of relief supplies to millions of starving people. As the operation progressed, we became aware that one of the main problems we faced was coming from a demented tribal warlord and his gangs of murderous thugs. Mohamed Fariq Adiz and his crew of narcotic-chewing killers were deliberately sabotaging and stealing United Nations food shipments, thereby ensuring that the genocide by starvation would continue. The United States took exception to this state of affairs, and the stage was set for the inevitable confrontation.

Why do these things happen?

On the 3rd of October 1993, 101 American soldiers launched a raid into the heart of Mogadishu with the intention of capturing Adiz and his top dogs. Initially, the mission went well, with 19 of the bad guys captured. Then a Blackhawk helicopter was shot down as it orbited above the battle, and the situation changed for the worse. In the hours that followed, the besieged U.S. troops fought a savage battle against a maniacal enemy that outnumbered them five to one. Despite taking heavy casualties, a normal occurrence in any ground confrontation, the Americans actually accomplished their mission and successfully withdrew, leaving behind thousands of dead and wounded enemy fighters. So badly did we hurt the Somali warlord that he and his surviving men actually abandoned their positions in downtown Mogadishu and hid out, praying that the Americans would not come at them again. A few months later we did what we do best. We ran away, sentencing that wretched land to more starvation and misery. Observing that latest example of U.S. cowardice was a young Saudi Arabian radical named Osama bin Laden.

In the years that followed our retreat from Somalia, we began to be plagued by a series of deadly terrorist attacks. Suicide bombers attacked the Navy destroyer U.S.S. Cole as it was refueling in Yemen, killing a number of American sailors and putting the warship out of commission. United States embassies in Kenya and Tanzania were bombed in a series of attacks that killed hundreds of innocent people. Our response to these incidents was to bluster and make vague threats to "bring the killers to justice." Not only did we not bring anyone to justice, we didn't do anything to anyone.

At the same time that we were busy sitting still for repeated terrorist attacks, we were playing a non-stop game of patty cake with Saddam Hussein. Saddam's troops regularly fired anti-aircraft missiles at U.S. and British planes patrolling the no-fly zones in northern and southern Iraq. Our response was predictable; we might drop a few bombs here or there or shoot a cruise missile or two, but that was about it. For fourteen years we played this silly game with the Baghdad madman while he gleefully slaughtered his own citizens and made billions off of the incompetence and corruption of the United Nations.

In the 1990's came another opportunity to show the world our lack of courage and resolve. The ongoing disintegration of the former Yugoslavia resulted in a situation of ethnic cleansing and genocide throughout the region. Mass graves were being filled, and the body counts reached epidemic proportions. The United States was again faced with the no-win situation of intervention vs. no intervention. Rather than making a solid decision and sticking with it, the U.S. chose the usual path. We partially intervened in some circumstances and in others we ignored the carnage. We dropped a few bombs and made some threats, but it soon became obvious to the rest of the world that we were afraid to do anything of real substance. The few times that we committed small contingents of ground troops, it was clear to both our friends and our enemies that America was scared to death of getting hurt. The possibility of taking casualties was something that we could not face. Even a six-week bombing campaign in Kosovo did little to rectify the situation, and nothing has really changed there to this very day.

On September 11, 2001, there came an attack that we could not ignore. Thousands of American citizens were dead and we had to do something. In the aftermath of the WTC attacks, America was swept by a wave of temporary patriotism and the outward appearance of resolve. Some of that patriotic display would have been nice to see before September 11th, but I guess that is beside the point. Now we were involved in a so-called "War on Terror" and feelings ran high. It was obvious from the start, however, that this situation would not last. After a relatively quick military victory in Afghanistan, the American public seemed ready to relax and go back to life as usual. When the President had the audacity to suggest that this conflict might not be over just yet, and that there were other tasks left to do, our resolve started to slowly unravel. The patriotic euphoria began to cool rapidly as it became apparent that this was a long-term situation and was not going to be wrapped up as quickly as people might have liked.

Why do these things happen?

The invasion of Iraq came next and again the United States was able to accomplish a rapid military victory. The destruction of Saddam Hussein's army came quickly and at a relatively low cost in American lives. The year following the fall of Baghdad, however, has not gone as smoothly. Unforeseen circumstances have arisen and we have run into various difficulties. I personally don't understand why anyone with half a brain would have thought that things would be any different, but evidently a large portion of the American populace thought exactly that. I guess real life is obligated to come off like some movie or something. Whatever the reason, as the situation in Iraq continues, the temporary resolve and courage of the American people are fading and fading fast. So, once again we are poised as a nation to do the one thing that we have continually shown the world that we are good at, running away.

If that is what we are like on the international front, how can the domestic front be any better? Our actions overseas are nothing more than a direct reflection of our attitudes and outlooks at home. If our usual action is to run away over there, how can it be any different over here? The average American citizen has been running for a long time.

When a neighborhood starts to have an increase in crime, the immediate answer is to run away. If there is a problem with the schools, grab your child and run away. When a criminal confronts you, give him what he wants and run away. When you have spent a lifetime being indoctrinated to not even consider the possibility of standing up for what is yours, the only answer left is to run.

In the months that followed September 11th, our desire to run away from our problems entered a new dimension. I have lost count of the number of people whom I have heard state a complete willingness to abandon all of our constitutional liberties in an effort to run away from the terrorist threat. "Forget the First Amendment," they say, "forget the second, forget them all! Just keep me safe and let me hide. Whatever happens, don't ask me to show any courage or a willingness to see things through, just keep me safe".

In the opinion of the international terrorist and the domestic criminal, the average American citizen is an easy mark who can be relied upon to put up little or no resistance when threatened. In light of our actions at home and abroad for the past fifty years, how could they have arrived at any other opinion?

Things were not always this way

We used to be a society renowned for its courage and tenacity; indeed, our nation was founded on the idea of defending what is ours. On the 19th of April 1775, thousands of ordinary Massachusetts citizens met and defeated two British infantry regiments along the narrow road from Concord to Boston, igniting a war of revolution. Despite many setbacks and horrific casualties, we stuck with the fight and after eight long years gained our independence. Our resolve was re-tested in 1812 when, once again, American citizens and soldiers faced down a British invasion and won.

From 1860 to 1865 the United States of America endured one of the most grueling tests that a nation can endure, a war with itself. For five years the very idea of our nation hung in the balance and the eventual outcome was always in doubt. Improvements in weaponry produced casualties on a scale never seen before, and the incompetence displayed by the early generals of the north resulted in a non-stop series of defeats and near defeats for the first two years of the conflict. Despite continuous bad news from the battlefront, the North held on and eventually crushed the Southern rebellion, restoring our nation.

After the civil war came a period of westward expansion as tens of thousands of citizens headed that way in search of a better life. What most of them found instead was danger and extreme hardship as they tried to establish themselves in a hostile land. Bullets, sickness, natural disasters, and other hazards killed thousands, but the rest hung on and more were always coming. The average citizen was not going to run away when things got bad, and by the late 1800's, the nation was established from ocean to ocean.

World War I was our first large-scale overseas commitment in a major conflict. Many Americans were against our involvement in the war, and the controversy continued throughout the hostilities. Once committed, however, we stuck it out and were victorious in the end. At the beginning of the Second World War, the average American citizen was again reluctant to venture into what most people considered a European conflict. At that point they were probably right, but obviously December 7, 1941, changed all that and once again, we were committed in a major struggle. Many dark days were endured by this nation during that conflict, and I am sure than in the mind of many it seemed as if it would go on forever. We stayed the course, however, and the world was immeasurably better for it.

For most of our history we have been looked upon as both a courageous nation and courageous individuals. If we are going to have any real security as a nation or as individuals, we will have to be looked upon that way again. If we are going to accomplish that goal, we are going to have to look closely at some of the factors that brought us to where we are now.

We are too self-critical for our own good

Introspection and self-criticism are good things to have in a society. The ability to look critically at our actions and ourselves is one of the things that make us different from the rest of the world. Taken too far, however, this quality will start to work against us and in the modern United States of America, we have taken it way too far. We have progressed from a state of healthy self-examination to a condition of destructive self-hatred. For the last thirty years, the liberal media and entertainment industry in this country have subjected our citizens to a non-stop barrage of ridicule and guilt. Over and over we are blasted with the subtle, and sometimes not-so-subtle, message that as Americans, all the bad things on this planet are somehow our fault. This has resulted in the formation of the "Blame America First," crowd and this insane outlook has come to dominate our political structure, news media, and entertainment industry. A sickening number of Americans have bought into this idea and as a result, we are far more worried about what people around the world think of us than we are about our own security and interests. This is one of the primary reasons that this nation is so ready and willing to run away from a commitment overseas. We turn on our television and see some foreign hypocrite moaning about how evil America is, and we are ready to agree with him. An anti-American statement is uttered and that is all that is necessary for that statement to be considered fact. When you see bumper stickers saying, "America had it coming" in reference to the September 11th attacks, you realize just how far this deranged viewpoint has penetrated our culture.

On the home front, if you happen to be a productive person lacking a criminal history, the message is that somehow the ills of this society are your fault. If you are a success in life, then it is your fault that there are those who are not, the message says. If you have achieved some financial headway, then all the poverty around you is because of you. If a crime is committed against you, then it is implied that the blame rests with you, the victim, and never with the perpetrator of the act. If you own a gun, then obviously all crimes committed with firearms are your fault. Millions of decent, law-abiding citizens have now come to feel a pointless sense of guilt over every aspect of their life. This lunacy has brought them to a state of stunned immobilization and has destroyed their ability to defend themselves from harm.

We are drowning in political correctness and American citizens are dead because of it

During the last twenty years, a new social phenomenon has crept into American life, and its effects have been devastating. The originators of this madness have even given it a name and that name sounds like it could have come right out of the communist manifesto. Begun on college campuses in the 1980's, the concept of "political correctness" has now spread its stain across the length and breadth of our societal structure. Completely disregarding the U.S. Constitution, university academics began to decree certain speech and viewpoints unacceptable. Obviously they had no legal authority to do this and still don't. However, it has been amazing to see how many ordinary citizens have fallen in line with this outright assault on their first amendment freedoms. At the core of this philosophy is the idea of symbolism over substance. In other words, if you don't like something, all you have to do is change the name and that will change its nature. A short man is now "height challenged" or something just as ridiculous. It is as if the most important thing in our society is not to look after day-to-day business; no, the most important thing in our society it is to make sure that nobody gets his or her feelings hurt.

The simple fact is that nowhere in the Constitution of the United States of America is there a guarantee that you can go through life without getting your feelings hurt. Sooner or later all of us will be misunderstood or insulted or both. This unfortunate incident may come about as a result of our ethnic or national heritage, our income level, personal activities, or physical stature. It's going to happen and there isn't much that we can do about it. Any attempt to regulate human behavior at that level is an exercise in futility. At best it accomplishes nothing and at worst it can be dangerous to individual citizens, yet our society in inundated with this phenomenon. The airline security procedures that came about in the aftermath of September 11th attacks serve as one of the best examples of what I have been saying. The procedures are fine in and of themselves; it is the way that they are carried out that is the problem.

I didn't have an opportunity to fly on a commercial airliner until eighteen months after the attack. When I did finally get a chance to take a business trip (to Seattle), I was disgusted at what I saw when it came to passenger security. Baton Rouge to Seattle wasn't too bad, pretty much business as usual. The return trip, however, was a bit different. As I passed through the boarding procedure, along with thousands of other travelers, it became readily apparent that the airport security personnel were busy looking for everyone except the enemy. During their supposed random searches I saw them stop and frisk a woman who had to be in her eighties, several children, just about any white male who looked like he did some sort of real work for a living, and some poor guy with one leg. While conducting these searches, the security folks maintained an irritating air of self-righteous arrogance, continually reminding all around them "this is for everyone's safety."

Now I was not all that concerned about flying on the same plane as the eighty-year-old woman who could barely walk. The kids were a bit irritating with all their running around and yelling, but I didn't feel any real danger from them. As far as all the working class white males, well most of them looked more like the kind of guy that would be more likely to come and fix my broken toilet than a guy who would hijack the plane that I was on. The guy with one leg didn't look like he could move fast enough to make the flight, much less do any harm to it. On the other hand, the four surly males of Middle Eastern descent who were hanging around the ATM machine did cause me a bit of concern, yet when they finally decided to come through the line, they were quickly passed through with no fanfare or fuss.

The truth of this matter is that the airport screeners were less afraid of a potential hijacker than they were of the perception that they were somehow unfairly profiling someone. Better a few

Why do these things happen?

thousand more innocent people die in a flaming pile than somebody feel singled out because of his or her ethic features, I suppose. I wish this insanity ended at the check-in line but unfortunately, it doesn't. Political correctness raises its ugly head in other domestic situations. Time and again there have been cases where the ethnicity of a rampaging killer has been kept from the public because those in charge of catching him were more afraid of being called racists than they were of his killing someone else. A shining example of this type of behavior on the part of the authorities was the Washington, D.C., and northern Virginia sniper saga. That one just had to be a "white male with an NRA sticker in his window," didn't it? Everybody knew that the very nature of this crime prohibited the involvement of any other racial group. The only problem with that though process was that it was totally wrong. The killers were black males in that case. We will never know how many times those murderers were able to kill and then escape the scenes of their crimes because the police and public were looking for a white male. Failing to release information of this type is an unconscionable act if it is done for any reason relating to political correctness.

You cannot exist as a human being on planet earth without irritating somebody along the way, so stop worrying about it. You are not responsible for what went on in this country before you were even born. In fact, you are not responsible for anything that has happened outside of your direct control. You can't go back in time and take credit for any of the good things that happened, so don't go back and try to take credit for the bad things. You have no obligation to be a victim of a crime because injustices were done to others. The Constitution is still in effect, and it is the law of the land, regardless of the insane mutterings of the political left.

We have to change the way we think

Things are not going to get any better until we change our viewpoint on a few issues. The War on Terror is nowhere near over and will not be for some time to come. We are not going to see an end to this conflict until our enemies realize that attacking us carries a higher price tag than they are willing to pay. Our enemies will never like us, but they can be made to respect and fear us. Only when they do that will be able to live with some real national security again. We are a long way from accomplishing that goal.

Time and time again, the news media sees fit to inform us how much we are disliked around the world and, time and time again, I ask the question, "Who cares?" The United States is not invalid as a nation and culture just because there are people out there who don't like us. Being scorned by others is no reason for this country to stop acting in its own best interest.

On a more personal level, the threat of a criminal attack on your person remains the single greatest threat that you face as an American citizen today. This situation will remain until the criminal element realizes that to attack the average citizen carries a higher price tag than they are willing to pay. The criminals will never like you but they can be made to respect and fear you. Only when that happens will you be able to live with some real personal security again. We are a long way from accomplishing that goal.

If we are going to accomplish either goal, we will have to change the way we think. Changing the way we think is the purpose of this book, so read on.

Chapter 3
Life and liberty; the gift from long ago

"You cannot claim to value something if you are not willing to defend it"

Kit Cessna

On the 19th of April 1775, a few thousand ordinary citizens of the Massachusetts Colony inflicted a stunning defeat on a world power. This confrontation set the stage for the creation of the nation and society that you now live in. All of the blessings and benefits that we enjoy today came about because of the incredible courage that they displayed on that terrible afternoon. It must be remembered, however, that these good folks did not face down the British Army that day because they wanted to ensure that we would live in freedom in the twenty-first century. In fact, the colonial militiamen were probably incapable of imagining the passage of that much time. Even if they could have seen into the future and viewed the results of that day's work, it is doubtful that they would have understood or cared. They did what they did because they had had enough of living under the heavy hand of an aristocracy that didn't even consider them fully human, a ruling authority that looked upon them at best as second-class citizens and, at worst, mere serfs. They had had enough of the Crown's complete disregard for their lives and property, and they set out to do something about it.

Whatever their individual reasons for participating in the events of that day, be it rage or vengeance, the colonial militiamen did not write the Constitution nor the Bill of Rights on the long road back to Boston. Even as they fought and died, they did not foresee a sovereign nation such as we now live in, and in fact most of them did not necessarily believe in the concept of independence at all. After the battle, the majority of the colonial combatants would have jumped at the chance to have things go back to the way they were before the first shot was fired. It was only in the hours and days after the fight that it dawned on them that the only road left open was the one to independence.

In taking that road to independence, those brave souls gave you and me a gift that endures to this present time. What they created among the flash and boom of their primitive weapons was the beginning of our nation, the beginning of the greatest civilization in the history of humanity. Yes, that is what I said and I will say it again without hesitation or embarrassment, the greatest civilization in the history of humanity. We are beholden to those folks for the actions that they took on that fateful day and we owe them everything. All that we have today is due to the raw courage that they displayed on that April afternoon and the eight brutal years that followed. Even after the final defeat of the British at Yorktown, we still did not have the nation that we have today. It took more than a decade of deliberation and argument for those magic words "We the people of the United States, in order to form a more perfect union" to appear on paper.

With the signing of that document, for the first time in history a republic was founded on the belief that the life of an individual belonged only to that individual. Our Constitution emphatically states that life is solely the asset of the individual who possesses it, and that conviction is the foundation of all the liberties that we now have. That had never happened before and has not happened since. This condition is unique in the history of mankind.

The history of mankind

The history of mankind is a history of brutality and oppression. Said another way: much of human history has been the story of an

Life and liberty; the gift from long ago

unwilling populace ruled by a series of tyrannical, psychopathic monsters. Call them whatever you want, be it Kings, Tsars, Caesars or The Party, they have all been pretty much the same. The raw ego and vanity of these folks is represented by the carpet of sun-bleached skulls and bones that stretched from the islands of Great Britain to the shores of China. All over the globe are physical reminders of this time; from the piles of square rocks gathering dust in the desert, to the vine-choked temples hiding in the jungles. Reminders of the way things were and in some cases the way they still are.

Certainly some of the accomplishments of these past civilizations can be admired-until you reflect upon the method by which they were accomplished. Gaze at the Pyramids of Giza and you will see the ghosts of tens of thousands of slaves who spent their entire lives piling up rocks so that some teenage king could have a splendid gravesite. The ruins of the Roman Coliseum echo with the screams of thousands who died for the entertainment of others, primarily the ruling class. Poke around the ruins of a Mayan temple and you are standing in a place where the blood of sacrifice victims was literally ankle deep on some days. The scattered castles throughout Europe are reminders of a time when all things belonged to the King or the religious authority that controlled him, and the life of the individual human being was held in little or no regard.

The average citizen of the past spent his short days in a state of official or unofficial bondage. Men and women toiled daily for subsistence, and those in power seized all else. Occasionally some royal or religious personage would incite a country to declare war on another people, and then the really pleasurable part of life would begin. Forcibly conscripted into standing armies, or simply gathered into smelly mobs and led by the same arrogant few who had abused them since their birth, they would set forth. If they were lucky, those who led them were not completely incompetent and brought them a victory or two, allowing some of them to stay alive. More than likely, those who led them led them straight to their graves. Whole armies would run out of food and water, and every last individual would die. In other cases, invading armies managed to alienate the local populace of the area that they occupied and ended up having to kill them all or be killed.

The more recent era has, unfortunately, been no different. At the time of Lexington and Concord the common citizens of most nations lived under an official system of slavery. Wealthy landowners and titled nobility literally owned the lives of those around them and treated them accordingly.

This situation continued into the twentieth century and culminated with the First World War. During the long blood-soaked years of that struggle, an entire generation of young European males was obliterated by artillery and machinegun fire in the name of the Archdukes and Kings. This catastrophe resulted in the world of royalty losing its place in the scheme of things as they began to be replaced by political parties. This process had actually started long before with the French Revolution, but now it took hold with a fury. What was to follow was even worse than what had passed, as the representatives of the "working man" took charge of the planet.

Scorning the efforts of the past, these "protectors of the people" ushered in a time wherein mass murder was finally taken seriously and given the all-out effort it deserved. Backed up by modern weaponry and unencumbered by Royal incompetence and inefficiency, the real killing could now begin, and so it did. Starting with the 1917 Russian Revolution, and spreading across Europe and Asia, this was the time for the common citizen to show the world that he was more efficient at collective homicide than any king or queen had ever been. Over the next several decades, these political ideologues struggled to change the basic make-up of the world. From a planet of kings and peasants they endeavored to create a domain of peasants. Blissfully slaughtering any and all who didn't fit their idea of the quintessential working class, they rid their societies of anyone with education, enthusiasm, and manners and slowly ground their populations into a shapeless gray mob. Layer after layer of fresh corpses was added to the centuries-old graveyard that is Europe and Asia.

This orgy of politically inspired murder culminated with the

Second World War, and in those years the level of government-inspired killing reached the highest point in human history. The end of that conflict brought about a fifty-year face-off between the few nations in the world that still had some semblance of freedom, primarily the United States, and an empire of totalitarian socialism that sought to spread itself across the globe. While this empire was economically defeated, the mindset, beliefs, and attitudes that brought it about are still very much alive in the rest of the world. That brings us to the present day.

The modern world

In some of the more modern, benevolent societies of today, the pretense of liberty is allowed to exist. Small insignificant freedoms are doled out by the governmental structure, and much is made of them. "Look at us," they proclaim. "We are a free society just like you Americans." Most of the European nations fall into this category, and at first glance there seems to be little difference in our cultures. The average British, French, or German citizens appear to lead an unfettered life much like their American counterparts. The average Japanese civilian has a few more restrictions than the European, but again appears to live a rather unrestrained existence.

However, a close examination of that day-to-day existence in those places will quickly show that this is not the case. Government interference and outright control of those nations' economies ensure that a large portion of the population wanders about in a permanent state of unemployment and frustration. Along with the high rate of joblessness, these government controls ensure astronomical prices on just about everything necessary for daily life. Despite their easier access to Middle Eastern oil, the European masses pay up to nine dollars a gallon for gasoline, most of which is government taxation. In some of these nations, heavy poll taxes effectively restrict the right to vote to those few who can afford it. There seems to be no real resistance to these circumstances and there is a simple reason for this condition. The European populace has made an unwritten, and in some cases written, deal with their respective governments. The basic verbiage of the agreement is as follows:

> *I the common citizen of (fill in appropriate European country) do hereby willingly and with great enthusiasm surrender all my individual liberties and freedoms to my respective government. I will forgo the responsibility for charting the course of my life, and allow others to make my decisions for me. In fact, I will even give up the most basic of rights, the right to adequately defend my person from violent attack. If I am unfortunate enough to cross paths with a person of evil intent, I will endeavor to die quietly so as to not upset the sensibilities of my fellow citizens. Without question, I will look to my ruling authority for all things, including the continuance of my existence.*
>
> *In return for this acquiescence, I make the following demands of that same government. First and foremost, I wish to live out my days wrapped snugly in a governmental financial cocoon. If I am lazy or incompetent and fail to get adequate education or job training, this shall have no direct consequences upon me. If I am foolish enough to work in an industry or trade that is becoming outdated, my lifestyle will not change for my government will step in with immediate subsidies to those same industries or trades. My health care will be free and on demand, relieving me of any responsibility to live a healthy life and/or plan for a future illness. At all times during the course of my existence I will demand more goods and services in return for less effort and productivity on my part. If I want a thirty-hour workweek, it will come about whether or not the current economic realities support it. If any of my fellow citizens have the gall to attempt to work harder than I, I will demand their immediate arrest and prosecution.*
>
> *At no time will my government allow me to be deprived of my illusions pertaining to my importance to the world in general. I*

Life and liberty; the gift from long ago

will sit arrogantly amid the scattered ruins of two thousand years of non-stop warfare, sipping wine and calmly reflecting on my superior level of sophistication. Casting general scorn upon all the other inhabitants of the planet, especially those uncultured upstarts across the Atlantic, I will maintain my superiority despite any evidence to the contrary. I will pay no recognition to the fact that two times in a single century, all of us world wise, cosmopolitan intellectuals of the European landmass tried our best to kill all of each other in one sitting. The ghosts of the millions of citizens of non-European nations who died after being dragged into both of these murderous escapades will not trouble my self-view.

Since I will not be separated from my personal fantasies of self-importance, I demand that my government create their own visions of glory. They will continually squawk to the rest of the world about our need to be consulted in every decision concerning the use of military force, all the while ignoring the fact that they have allowed their own militaries to shrink into insignificance. My government will shrilly demand to be treated as a super power even though we are no longer capable of protecting our own shores from invasion, much less projecting any useful level of force elsewhere. While foreign and domestic terrorist groups operate among us unhindered, killing thousands of our own citizens over the years, my government will stand ready to pour criticism on any other nation that has the audacity to try and stop the carnage.

I will consider it to be perfectly normal that tens of thousands of young, able bodied males in my society spend their spare time dying their hair purple and rampaging through soccer stadiums, crushing innocent people to death, while young Americans of the same age are busy soaking up bullets and mine fragments in my own backyard in a series of little vicious ethnic wars that were our creation to begin with. When their flag-draped coffins are unloaded at home, I will watch on CNN and sneer self-righteously, calling them "Cowboys." Last, but *not least, if I eventually tire of government-enforced mediocrity and borderline poverty, I will immediately flee to the United States and avail myself to any and all benefits provided by that embarrassingly inferior culture. Having landed on their shores, I will launch into an unrelenting campaign of verbal sarcasm directed at everything around me. I will tirelessly struggle to educate those barbarians around me as to the superiority of the culture that I fled from. Once I have received a good education at a reasonable price and have obtained a standard of living and economic status that I would not have accomplished back home in ten thousand years, I will lose no opportunity to denounce, insult and destroy from within the very society to which I owe everything that I now have.*

The Europeans are not the only ones who have made such a deal with their rulers; much of the rest of the world has a similar arrangement. Total control has been surrendered to the government and in some places that control can reach extreme levels. A few years ago the government of Brazil decided that they didn't have enough money to continue business. They decided to make up for this shortfall by raiding the savings accounts of the average Brazilian citizen. Now the government of that developing nation would, no doubt, be the first ones to claim that the freedoms enjoyed by their citizens are equal to any other society. This did not stop them, however, from stealing the life savings of millions of Brazilians. Can you imagine the resulting uproar if that had been tried here? I would submit that any government that doesn't believe that your hard-earned money belongs to you certainly doesn't believe that your life belongs to you either.

Oil-rich Middle Eastern states brag about a standard of living for their people that has in some cases surpassed that of the western nations, the United States included. Keep in mind, though, that in that part of the world, you literally can be arrested, convicted, and executed if the ruling authority believes that you are even thinking about doing something wrong. The city streets in these countries are crowded with thousands of expensive vehicles, and palace-like

Life and liberty; the gift from long ago

villas dot the landscape. Medical care is free and tens of thousands of foreign servants are there to perform all the daily tasks of the society. As a result, most citizens of these nations have no real responsibly and live lives of complete idleness. They all know, however, that they have nothing that was not given to them by the ruling power. As one young man from Kuwait told me "What is given today will be taken tomorrow." Notice that he did not say, "may be taken," he said, "will be taken." This was a highly educated citizen of that nation, and his family's connections to the Emir guaranteed him a life of ease and luxury. As a member of middle class America, my standard of living did not begin to compare with his, yet I wish that you could have heard the bitterness and envy in his voice as he compared his life to mine. "You're lucky" he said. "You got to earn what you have and it actually belongs to you."

Some nations make no pretense on this issue and straightforwardly proclaim that the lives of their citizens are theirs to do with as they please. Ordinary civilians live under a permanent cloud of suspicion and may be arrested or detained at any time. North Korea is a fine example of this condition, and the citizens of that nation function as little more than slaves to the central Communist authority. In that "workers paradise" you receive your job assignment at a young age, and the job is over on the day that you die. You can end up sweeping the streets or toiling in a freezing coal mine for decades. If you are male, that privilege only comes after a long brutal tour in the military, where you exist on the edge of starvation and are repeatedly informed that one day you will be lucky enough to sacrifice your life to the glorious cause of "scientific socialism."

In some cases no societal structure exists to begin with. Even now in the beginning of the new century, a large portion of this earth is under the rule of warring tribal factions. From the mountains of Afghanistan to the former Yugoslavia, small tribal groups slash and claw at each other for possession and power, and the savagery and brutality of these groups is legendary. Huge military invasions, loosely described as peacekeeping missions, are unable to do anything about the murder and carnage. This type of venture only serves to guarantee a steady trickle of needless military casualties from the country dumb enough to get involved in the first place. Even outright military assaults, such as what happened in Afghanistan after September 11th, have had no real impact on the thought processes of these cultures. The life of the unfortunate average person in these lands never has been and never will be worth anything to those in power.

Time and time again on the African continent, tribal wars have claimed hundreds of thousands of lives at a whack. Whole villages are exterminated for no other reason than the inhabitants being silly enough as to be caught descending from the wrong bloodline. The continuous fighting destroys what little economy they have and throws hundreds of thousands into a condition of starvation. These same starving people are then ruthlessly shot down as they try to receive from other nations, primarily the United States, the food shipments that were meant for them in the first place. The structure of those societies depends solely upon which of the many warlords is the most vicious and well armed, for these are the ones who claim the food and anything else worth having.

It is important to remember that in all of these societies that I have described, there are a privileged few who enjoy personal freedoms that actually surpass those of the average American citizen. These lucky ones get to do just about anything that comes to their minds. If their religion prohibits certain activities, such as alcohol consumption or sexual deviances, they just hop a plane to New York or some other equally tempting site and have at it. If they hearken from a socialist or communist enclave, they usually manage to find their way to Saks Fifth Avenue for a little shopping spree in the heart of capitalism. Freedom for them is total and unrestricted and it will last as long as they are on the side of the current power structure. The moment that they either abandon or are perceived to abandon that structure, they will be introduced to the deprived existence of their less-powerful countrymen. If they are lucky that is all that will happen to them; more than likely, though, they will end up in a prison cell or in a ditch with a bullet in their head. If they are swift enough to escape the vengeful designs of their government, most of them come running to the one place that they have always claimed to despise, the good old USA. Once here, they will unhesitatingly avail themselves of every benefit this society has to offer, all the while claiming to ache for the "homeland."

If it sounds as if I'm not very impressed with the other nations of this world, it's because I'm not. I have been to over sixty of them during the course of my life and I became very familiar with the structures and values of their societies. The differences between them and us would make for a long, long list and are too numerous to count. The main difference, and the most profound one, as I see it, is with the basic values of those varied systems. In all cases the individual citizen is at best considered a mere asset of the government. At worst, he is someone to be bullied, terrorized, and enslaved. Most governments on this earth will at one time or another pay lip service to the idea of individual freedom, but that is usually as far as it goes. Even in the rare cases in which a ruling power decides to grant some actual liberties, there are many strings attached and, sooner or later, those strings are going to get yanked. One place on planet earth is different and remains different despite efforts by some of its own leaders and citizens to change it. That place is the United States of America. Here, unlike any other place, your existence belongs to you and only you.

Your life belongs to you, not the government

Although it can be taken from you after due process of the law, your life doesn't belong to the government. It never has and hopefully never will. However, one should be aware that certain members of that same institution might attempt to argue with you on that point. By their very nature, government institutions tend to be abusive of their power and there has never been one that has not, on occasion, treated the lives of its citizens with callous disregard. This includes our own power structure, although they have the best track record so far. The basic truth is that a governmental structure cares very little for the individual lives of those under its control. Notice that I said "individual lives," not the lives of the population as a whole. A government can and usually will commit all its resources to protect the masses, but it will not get all that serious about single citizens. There is no way that it can, really. With hundreds of millions of people to be concerned about, the mere individual fades into insignificance.

I'm not conducting an anti-government tirade here, and I don't believe in the conspiracy theories that abound these days. I don't buy into the popular notion that holds that there is a dark, malignant group of plotters in Washington, D.C., who spend all their hours scheming about ways to deprive you of your life and liberties. I have spent my entire adult life in one form of government service or another, and I can assure you that the "black helicopters" are not flying. A collusion of that complexity and magnitude is beyond the capability of a human government to pull off. Based on their record so far, if the bureaucrats in Washington, D.C., actually tried to deprive you of your freedoms, you would end up with even more of them than you have now. Remember this, however, that while those in power are not actually trying to hurt you, they are not looking out for you either. Nobody in authority is spending any time worrying about whether or not you see the sun come up tomorrow. Not even the politicians that fill your television screen every day with their five hundred dollar haircuts and bulging bank accounts have any concern for you as an individual. How could they?

Governments play a numbers game with every endeavor that they perform. I don't believe that in most cases this is done with any malice or ill will; it is just the way that they do business. The cold, hard fact of the matter is this: they don't have a stake in your survival. If they bothered to think about it, those in power would really rather that you didn't get killed as a result of their activity or inactivity. If you do get killed as a result of something that they did or did not do, as individuals, they may even feel bad about what happened, but it will probably have no direct impact on them as a person. Their life will go on and if they bore no direct responsibility for your demise, their job will also go on. Learn to live with that simple fact and the world around you will come into sharper focus. It's nothing to moan about, it's just the way it is.

Governments are an absolutely necessary institution on this planet. Without them confusion and anarchy would reign, and life would be very short and unpleasant for the average individual. Necessary though they may be, they are neither your parent nor your guardian. The governmental structure is, by its very nature, incapable of caring about your life as an individual. Only you can do that, so why should they own that life instead of you?

Your life belongs to you, not the "people"

Your existence does not belong to "society" or "the people," and the sheer numbers of horrific acts that have been justified in the name of those two faceless entities boggle the mind. Starting with the French Revolution and continuing with the now extinct Union of Soviet Socialist Republics, there has been enough innocent blood spilled by the disciples of this ideology to spread a stain across the entire planet. From the thump of the guillotine in eighteenth century Paris to the enforced starvation of millions under the Georgian dictator, "Comrade Joe Stalin," there has been a continuous wave of criminal acts committed in the name of the masses.

Put whatever labels on it that you want, socialism or communism, the results are always the same. Actually, in my Random House College Dictionary the description of these two supposedly different forms of government is identical. Whatever it's called, the institution of this ideology into a societal structure practically guarantees a session of mass murder, sooner or later. Under this type of administration, all property is said to be the property of the population as a whole. That includes the life of the individual citizens who make up the society. The theory is that all things are owned equally and will be distributed equally. Like a lot of theories, this one has never actually worked. What happens instead is that all things are owned and controlled by a central authority that claims to represent the populace. What the central authority actually represents is itself and, once in power, it will spend most of its time trying to ensure that it remains in power. Suspicion and paranoia are the hallmarks of such a government, and anyone who is thought to be in opposition is treated harshly. Eventually, the central authority will come to see all of its citizens as potential threats, and the massacres will follow soon thereafter.

For those of you who would attempt to inform me that not all nations who call themselves "socialist" have gone down this road, I would point out a simple economic fact. Calling yourself something does not make you that something. Many of the nations that refer to themselves in these terms are actually practicing free market capitalism at some level. One the other hand, every society that has had a pure form of this type of ruler ship has suffered the same fate, government sponsored mass murder.

Your life belongs to you, not the church

Your life doesn't belong to the church, for the time has long passes wherein religious organizations held that level of power in western culture. This is a good thing and we all should be thankful for this, regardless of our religious convictions. There has never in history been a religious organization that held as its primary belief that the life of the common individual belonged solely to him or her. History shows us that, as institutions, religious organizations can be brutal in the extreme and act with total disregard toward individual lives under their influence. Since the beginning of humanity, there has been an unbroken series of horrific acts committed in the name

Life and liberty; the gift from long ago

of some sort of higher power. The Christian Crusaders cut a river of blood a thousand miles wide through the then known world. In medieval Europe, holding unauthorized views on religious matters could and did get you subjected to acts of torture that would have made Hannibal Lector jealous.

For the past sixty years, radical followers of Islam have waged a war with each other and the predominantly Christian West. I cannot remember a time in my life that I could not turn on the television or pick up a newspaper and see or read about those people killing each other. From simple assassinations to bombings to massive terrorist attacks, the carnage goes on. Every time there is an attempt at peace and reconciliation, something happens to blow the chance. Ruling political structures on both sides of this issue make no real attempt to stop it and, why should they? Both sides have a vested interest in seeing the bloodshed continue indefinitely.

In the Gaza Strip and the West Bank area, terrorist leaders ruthlessly prey on youngsters whom they brainwash and send on suicide missions. Children of both sexes, barely into their teenage years, wrap their bodies with explosives and set off on their one-way trip to a theoretical paradise. Upon reaching their intended target, be it a crowded bus or restaurant, they detonate the device, and dozens are killed and wounded. Night after night we are witness to the shrieks of ambulances and the vacant stares of the bloody survivors.

Religious radicals on the other side of the issue have hands that are just as bloody. For decades, in acquiescence to the Jewish Orthodox population, the Israeli government has fed the flames with non-stop construction of Jewish settlements located in traditionally Palestinian areas. The existence of these isolated enclaves guarantees a never-ending series of bloody confrontations between protesting Arab youths and the Israeli troops sent in to protect the settlements. Teenage Israeli conscripts shoot down the rock-throwing protesters and are sometimes themselves killed in the clashes. Israeli Army bulldozers level dozens of houses a week, ostensibly in retaliation for acts of terror committed by suspected residents of those structures. At least that is the reason given for these acts of destruction but, it is interesting to note how many small Israeli settlements spring up on the now cleared sites. It never seems to stop, and it seems that it never will.

All over the Middle East and the Persian Gulf, terrorist organizations proclaiming to act on behalf of God recruit hundreds of individuals to their ranks. These zealots are sent off to training camps where they are taught the fine art of organized murder and then sent forth to places like Afghanistan and Iraq to fight the non-believers. Most of them are eventually killed, but I suppose that just makes room for the next batch to follow. Some of these maniacs receive a level of training that allows them to penetrate the western countries, and days like September 11th are the result. All in the name of God.

I am not conducting an anti-religious tirade here, but I feel it necessary to point out a few obvious facts. Religion certainly has its place in any culture. A belief in a higher power seems to be universal among mankind and to me that is logical and justified. As I look around me everyday I see the direct evidence of a creator; nothing else makes any sense. However, unlike most people of religious faith, I have come to the point where I completely separate my belief in a higher power from my views on religious institutions here on earth. As far as I am concerned, they are two completely separate subjects and have only occasionally shared the same goals. On one side is a supremely benevolent being that wishes for us to live in peace and freedom and use our lives as we see fit. On the other side are ancient institutions that care nothing for the individuals in their ranks and only wish to use up those lives as the institution sees fit.

Under the laws of this nation, your God-given existence belongs to you and you only, and it cannot be arbitrarily claimed by anyone else, including the so-called representatives of that same God.

Your life belongs to you, not a criminal

If your life doesn't belong to the government, the people, or the church, then it certainly doesn't belong to some murdering criminal either. If those powerful institutions can make no legitimate claim to your life, then how can some low-life thug? The criminal element in our society has no right to your life or anything else that is yours. This is true regardless of the personal circumstances of any criminal. The criminal doesn't have a claim on your life even if he is down on his luck or has had a bad childhood. His daddy not loving him enough or the priest loving him too much gives him no right to take away your existence. Even being a victim of racial injustice, both real and imagined, gives him no justification to deprive you of anything, much less your life.

Assign your life proper value

The average American citizen enjoys a life of liberty and freedom that has never before been seen on this planet. Certainly we have laws that govern day-to-day existence; we could not be a civilized society without those regulations. In comparison to other societies, both past and present, the codes of our civilization are unrestrictive in the extreme. Under these laws we are able to lead pretty much whatever kind of life we wish. It is up to us really; we are free to reach as high or low as we can imagine. In our system some people win big in the game of life, some are average, and some below average. We are not necessarily guaranteed success in our ventures, which are subject to a number of different factors, some of which we control and others we do not. Attitude, talent, education, perseverance, and plain luck all play a part in what we make of our existence. Thanks to those brave colonials long ago, we all have the opportunity to try.

Ladies and gentlemen, this book is about changing your outlook on life so that you will be able to survive a violent attack. Changing a basic outlook on life is one of the most difficult endeavors that a human being can undertake. It is hard, and there is no way to make it easy. However, when you undertake such a task, it is helpful to examine your core values and decide if they work or don't work. From that examination, you may be able to come up with a new set of values and these convictions will help you on your journey. The most basic value that you should have in your life is that life itself. If you assign that life its proper value and keep that value in mind always, your path will be much easier. Before you read any further, go and look at yourself in the mirror. While looking yourself in the eye, decide that your existence has real worth and remember that as you proceed through the rest of the book.

Chapter 4
Developing a stay-alive mindset

"When possible make decisions now, even if the action is in the future. A reviewed decision is usually better than one reached at the last moment."

William B. Given, Jr.

"It does not take much strength to do things, but it requires great strength to decide on what to do."

Elbert Hubbard

American philosopher and writer 1856-1915

There has been a common expression in military circles that says, "It is not the weapon that counts a much as the man using it." A more quaint way of putting it is that "its not the size of the dog in the fight that makes the difference but the size of the fight in the dog." Military history is replete with examples of poorly equipped but motivated forces prevailing over a well equipped, but poorly motivated adversary. In these situations the mindset and motivation of the individual fighter was far more important than his arms or equipment. The first three years of the American Civil War are a shining example of this basic truth. A ragtag Southern Army, armed with an unshakable belief in the rightness of their cause and the inevitability of victory, defeated the Union forces in battle time and time again. These victories should have been impossible for the rebels to accomplish as the army of the North enjoyed an overwhelming advantage in men and equipment. For every barefoot infantryman marching for the South, there were no less than five well-trained and well-equipped Union soldiers opposing him. Along with an abundance of soldiers, muskets and cannon, the North possessed a modern navy that had achieved the status of a world power. This armada was able to place an economic stranglehold on the seceding states from the start of the war.

Faced with these odds, the Confederate Armies should have been crushed in the first few weeks of the conflict. Instead, they defeated their blue-coated foes on battlefield after battlefield in a series of victories that lasted for almost three years. There is no other plausible explanation for this than the mind-set of the southern soldier and his commanders. The rebel soldier believed that he could win and win he did. It wasn't until the summer of 1863, on a hilltop outside a small Pennsylvania farm town, that the northern soldier began to develop that same mindset, and the course of history changed.

That is a historical example but it is pertinent to our lives today. Develop the right mindset, and you will have a much better chance at survival even if the odds are seemingly against you.

What is a mindset?

"You are today where your thoughts have brought you; you will be tomorrow where your thoughts take you."

James Allen

The dictionary describes a mindset first as "an intention or inclination" and secondly as "a disposition or mood." In everyday terms, a mindset is nothing more than the anticipation of a set of circumstances and making preliminary plans to deal with those circumstances. An attitude, if you will, about a possible future occurrence. For a citizen facing the current criminal threat, a proper mindset is absolutely critical to your future survival. The way you think about a situation is directly related to how you will perform in that same situation

If you take a good look at your daily life, you will find that you have developed a mind-set about many things. Having an insurance policy is a good example of planning for a possible future event. Getting an education, saving money, and buying a house are some more. In all of these examples, forethought and anticipation of future events are the key to your individual attitude or mindset. Based on that, you might think that making plans to defend your life in the face of a deadly attack would be another commonly held mind-set. Unfortunately, that is not the case and, in fact, the average American citizen has no mindset or preparation whatsoever when it comes to self-defense.

The mindset of the average American today; call somebody to come save me

"You cannot surrender your way to safety."

Kit Cessna

In modern American society we handle very few of our own problems. When trouble comes, we just pick up the phone and turn the difficulty over to a member of that mythical, magical caste, "the professional." Contact the right member of this group and the problem will disappear, never to trouble you again. If there is a fire in your kitchen, call someone and maybe they will get there before the house collapses in a red-hot pile. If a maddened criminal threatens you, holler on your cell phone and maybe someone will intervene before you are killed. Whatever you do, don't take any action on your own, as you are not qualified to do anything except wait to be taken care of.

This total reliance on a professional reaction to your troubles is the mainstay of an already existing mindset in this country when it comes to facing a criminal attack. It is the basis of any official discussion by law enforcement on the subject of confrontation with a criminal. I call this philosophy the "give them whatever they want and rely on somebody to come and save you syndrome," and it has been ingrained into our culture over the last four decades. In other words, a total surrender to the aggressor. If somebody wants something of yours, you just give it to him and that's it. The basic theory is that if you simply surrender your physical property, you are more likely to survive the encounter than if you resist the theft.

A couple of generations of police officers have been forced to stand in front of groups of citizens across this nation and preach this view of life. These gatherings are usually held in a library or meeting hall and occur during some sort of crime spree. This flurry of lawlessness could be something relatively benign, like a series of daytime break-ins, or it could be something more heart stopping, like a serial killer lurking about. After being formally introduced, the officer of the evening would rise, adjust his gun belt, gaze at the assembled suburbanites, and solemnly regurgitate the official line on citizens versus crime. His all-knowing look would wash over the attendees as he espoused the virtues of deadbolt locksets and the value of trimming your hedges. Installation of floodlights around your home and the necessity of looking in the back seat of your car before entering would be elaborated on. If directly confronted, it was said, the standard course of action was not to resist. Just give them what they want and they will go away without harming you was the theory.

In these encounters there was one question that was hardly ever asked and, even if it was asked, it was never directly answered. The question is logical, however, and deserving of an answer. What if your criminal of the day was not there to steal your stereo? What if

Developing a stay-alive mindset

he had no interest in your television set or your silverware? What if his reason for confronting you in that darkened parking lot was not to relieve you of your automobile? What if he had no interest in your worldly goods and instead was after something a lot more valuable, like your life? What if he just wanted to kill you instead? What were you, the officially helpless citizen, supposed to do then?

Even if the conversation were somehow forced onto this unpleasant issue, the official answers from the representative of the law were usually vague and noncommittal. The unspecific response would contain references to some unnamed study, which had shown that your best bet in this deadly face-off was to surrender. In a few instances certain defensive techniques, such as karate chops and car keys in the eyeballs, got some lip service. Sometimes the lecturing cop brings along an assistant to demonstrate some of these miraculous cures, and the audience is subjected to a series of choreographed moves that are proposed to be the answer to any and all encounters. Nowhere is the truth of the matter stated, that truth being the fact that any unarmed combat technique requires years of practice and discipline in order to have even a small chance of being successfully employed, and therefore is irrelevant when it comes to self-defense for the average citizen.

The few times that the issue of a citizen defending him or herself with deadly force was raised, the reaction of the representative of law enforcement has been lukewarm at best. In most cases this option is dismissed out of hand, as the lecturing officer explains to you that you are simply not capable of conducting such an extreme level of defense. Speaking as if he was conversing with a room full of grade school children, he will deride the very idea of defense by lethal force. This option, he will grimly state, is reserved for that small group of beings called professionals. "Leave the guns to the pros," he will say. "We are, after all, trained to handle them." The message is clear; if you are not one of us, don't even think about this option.

During the decades of the sixties and seventies, this surrender mind-set crept into every part of our culture. Suddenly to be helpless in the face of a rampaging felon was portrayed to be trendy and cool. It was now intellectual and sophisticated to be the victim of a mugging in New York City, and the television waves were inundated with sitcoms containing characters who blithely considered this crime to be just one of the facets of life in the Big Apple. Woven through the story line of these productions was the message that to stand up and defend yourself from criminal attack was somehow wrong and narrow-minded. Having a knife or gun rammed into your face by some psychotic delinquent was almost like a badge of honor among the characters of these nightly make believes. I'm not kidding about this. Episodes of "Maude," "The Jefferson's," "All in the Family," and others preaching this viewpoint are in my memories of my adolescent and teenage years. In these performances, the surrender solution was driven home again and again. Any character who tried to suggest that this attitude of total capitulation might not be the best idea was subject to derision from all sides and eventually made to see the error of his ways.

In this world you tend to reap what you sow and the consequences of the "just give them what they want" mindset were clearly demonstrated on the morning of September 11th, 2001. When Islamic terrorists hijacked their aircraft, hundreds of American citizens did just that; they sat still and gave the criminals what they thought they wanted. Without a doubt, the occupants of those three ill-fated flights thought that if they offered no resistance, they would end the day shaken but still alive. It was not until the last few horrifying seconds of that encounter that it became clear that what the hijackers wanted was for everyone, including themselves, to be dead. A violent and fiery death is what those people received, all of them ending up as part of a burning pile of debris and corpses that took a year to clean up. On that sad day, we paid a heavy price for our "give up" frame of mind. In my opinion, there will be more of these attacks in the future.

Don't think for a minute that the local criminal population views us any differently than the international terrorists do. They know the psychological make-up of the average citizen better than our enemies

Developing a stay-alive mindset

abroad. They know that when they set out to find a helpless victim to rob or kill, they will be successful in their search. The September 11th hijackers found such an amendable group of American citizens on those ill-fated flights for the same reason that the Baton Rouge serial killer found such an easy array of victims. As a populace, we have abdicated our individual responsibility for our continued existence. I am talking about the inherent responsibility of a human being to be willing and able to defend his or her life. Individuals aside, the average American citizen of today possesses some of the worst survival skills in human history. There has never been a more helpless population anywhere at anytime that I can think of. Not only are their survival skills poor to non-existent, they have been exposed to a lifetime of indoctrination that prevents them from even thinking or conversing clearly on the issue. Does that sound bad? Well, it is, but it gets worse.

Of the entirety of the different social, economic, and political sectors that make up our modern culture, no group is more unprepared to deal with a life or death encounter than the average college-educated female. You will notice that I didn't attach any racial qualifiers to this statement. That is because those qualifiers are irrelevant. These unfortunate individuals have been indoctrinated into an attitude of helplessness that surpasses all others in our society and all others in our nation's history. Not only are these ladies totally incapable of competently defending themselves against a violent criminal attack; they are not even able to logically discuss the possibility of such an encounter. The indoctrination and outright brainwashing that has been performed on this segment of out nation is incredible. If you doubt my word I will simply direct you to the vast array of nightly sit-coms splashed across the television. The female characters portrayed in these presentations are sickeningly ignorant of the realities of the world that they live in and are born victims. They are no more able to defend themselves against an attack than a newborn child. Along with these make-believe episodes are the endless talk shows that further serve as a direct indoctrination session against the very idea of adequate self-defense. The college-educated female is the most likely group in our society to model their lives after the characters that they see on television. Millions of them have done so, and thousands of them have died because of it. Unfortunately, these women will continue to be victims until they change the way they think on this subject.

Developing a new mindset:

Step-One: Value your life and take responsibility for your own defense.

"They that are on their guard and appear ready to receive their adversaries are in much less danger of being attacked than the supine, secure and negligent."

Benjamin Franklin

"If you fail in your effort to stay alive, all your other endeavors are pretty much immaterial, aren't they?"

Kit Cessna

When it comes right down to it, the only thing that we can really say that we own is our individual existence. Material wealth can be temporary and even if is not, you have to be alive to enjoy it. Simply said, being alive is inherent to everything else that you will have or do. If you are going to develop a mindset for survival, you must assign your life its proper value. Part of assigning that value is the willingness on your part to defend that life and defend it with lethal force, if necessary. If you don't properly value you existence, then you cannot expect others to.

Developing a stay-alive mindset

As you read this, a logical question might be forming in your mind. "What about the police? Isn't my personal safety their responsibility? After all, what do we pay them for." An excellent question, and the answer goes right to the heart of the point I am attempting to make in this chapter. The truth in this case is unpleasant to face, but face it you must if you are going to develop a realistic outlook on this matter.

When it comes to the police, the facts of the matter are simple. It is not possible for any police department to provide direct protection for the mass of individuals under its jurisdiction. In reality, this task is not even a legal responsibility of the folks in blue. Their day-to-day job consists of keeping order, enforcing the law, and protecting public property. You don't hear your name mentioned anywhere in there do you? That's right, boys and girls (and especially you girls); the people with the guns and badges don't have the official mission of protecting you from harm. They never have had this task and probably never will. The reason for this is not because they don't care about you or because they are unconcerned with the effect of crime in the community. Nor is the reason that they don't want to stop the actions of the criminals. They are not directly responsible for your life and limb because there is no reasonable way that they can be held responsible. To protect each and every citizen from danger twenty-four hours a day would be a physical impossibility for an institution, no matter how dedicated. If you don't believe me, let's just do a little math.

Let's say, for example, that you live in a city of three hundred thousand citizens. That means that your police department numbers around six hundred or so. Now that doesn't mean that at any given moment there are six hundred officers on the street, so let's start subtracting. Of that six hundred there are probably around two hundred assigned as first responders to any incident. These will be in the uniformed patrol division, and they are the ones daily visible to the average citizen. The rest of the department is occupied with other tasks. The leadership structure of the organization requires a certain number of people to provide command and control. Others are in the investigative sections such as homicide and burglary. Some are working in the administrative areas grinding through the mounds of paperwork required by modern law enforcement. There may exist some specialized units such as bomb disposal, narcotics interdiction, and SWAT, and they will eat up even more warm bodies. For the most part, these people work a five-day week and have the weekends and holidays off. During the height of an average business day, it could be said that some of them would be available for response to a major incident, but after five p.m., they are gone for the day.

So, let's go back to the two hundred in uniform; in fact, we will be generous and make it two hundred and fifty. That's still not too bad, you say? Two hundred and fifty badge carriers spread out across the length and breath of the township ought to provide some level of protection for the individual, shouldn't it? Maybe it would if that were the actual number out there on the street hunting criminals, but we still need to do more math. As with other professions, cops work in shifts, so let's cut that number in thirds and that takes us down to eighty or so. They also get vacation time and days off, so we are now down to fifty something and I wish I could tell you that it ends there, but it doesn't. As in other professions of this type, police officers periodically go to training schools. These learning sessions last from a week to several weeks and are generally held out of town. So what we are left with in a city of three hundred thousand is something less than fifty officers on the street at any given time. These are the ones who are tasked to make a first response to any type of incident involving a citizen, and we really can't stop subtracting even here. Someone has to man the desk in each district or precinct so the number keeps falling. As far as the ones out there patrolling, well, they will respond if called and this will serve to temporarily drop the number even lower. If they make an arrest, then it takes time to take the prisoner to jail and book him in. If they are working an accident, then they are pretty much tied up with that, especially if there are injuries or fatalities. A juicy domestic dispute call may use up half a dozen units while the officers try to separate the warring factions.

Developing a stay-alive mindset

Given all these circumstances, it is possible that during any given day and night there are time periods wherein the number of officers actively patrolling your part of the city is zero. Think about that the next time that someone tries to tell you that your personal safety is solely in the hands of law enforcement.

Regardless of how many cops are actually out there, the thing that you must keep in mind is the number of them who are out there with the specific assignment of keeping you, the individual, alive. By specific assignment I mean a legally binding responsibility that, if not carried out, will result in criminal or civil action against the officer whose job it was to keep you from being dead. The simple answer to that question is, again, zero. None of these people put on their uniform and gun belt with that responsibility resting on their shoulders.

I'm not knocking the police, and civilization would not long survive without their presence. There are institutions in our society that exist solely to be called upon in the event of trouble and, if you are in trouble, you should call them. You would be rightfully thought of as a fool were you to refuse to call the fire department as your house burned down around you. Even more foolish, would be to refrain from calling the police when someone is trying to break into your home in the wee hours of the morning. These organizations are in place to provide a response to those occurrences. If you dial 911 and tell the dispatcher that you are soon to be a homicide victim, believe me they will come running. Arriving in time to stop a murder in progress is an occurrence that most police officers dream about. If you dial the fire department amid a background of crackling flames, they will be rolling out the door before the conversation is finished. So call them if you need to, just realize that they are human beings also and not supermen. The bottom line is this: nobody has as much of a vested interest in keeping you alive as you do. Therefore the primary individual responsible for your continued existence is you. Just as you are responsible for all the other day-to-day aspects of you life, you are also responsible to maintain that life in the face of a deadly threat.

Developing a mind-set:

Step-Two: Accept the fact that there are some bad people in this world.

"I would do the same thing again knowing that death row was waiting for me."

Convicted Murderer Jack Trawick

Writing to the Internet from an Alabama Prison

"Small crimes always precede great ones."

Jean Baptiste Racine

A commonly held view in modern America, at least among certain groups, is that there is no such thing as a totally bad person. It is as if it has now been deemed that the existence of such a creature is some sort of impossibility. Holders of this viewpoint would have you believe that any given person is only a product of their environment and past experiences and that base personality plays no part in their make-up. Well, boys and girls (and again especially you girls), I have been around and I am here to tell you different. Not only is there such a thing as a totally bad person, there are more of them around then you might like to think. They are with us now and have always been with us. There are people among us who have no redeeming qualities whatsoever. Nothing about them is good by any stretch of the imagination. These individuals were evil the day they came into this world and they will be evil all the days that they are here. They are just plain bad and no belief system on your part will change that simple fact.

Developing a stay-alive mindset

Call them sociopaths if you will, call them anti-social if you must. Put whatever label on them that you desire, but it will not change the reality of what goes on in their brains. I suppose that it can be argued that there are some people out there among the criminal class who are not totally evil. There are some of these folks who have internal barriers that they will usually not cross. I emphasize the word "usually," because time and time again people have ended up dead in circumstances wherein it was not the original intent of the criminal to kill them. It just kind of worked out that way, I guess. In any event, the point is rather immaterial for the simple reason that in a face-to-face encounter, you will not be able to tell the difference, will you?

For some reason, no discussion of these monsters seems complete without someone asking the "why" question. "Why are these people the way they are, and what makes them do the things they do?" While I am sure that there are many answers to this question, I am also sure that none of them are complete. Psychologists will tell you one thing, corrections officials will tell you something else. Politicians will put their two cents in (and that's about what their views are usually worth.) Nowhere will you find the clear-cut, definitive answer that you are seeking. I have come up with my own answer, though, and it is brutally simple. These folks do the things that they do because they like doing them. When a serial killer cuts some helpless woman to pieces, he is not doing it because he doesn't enjoy it. On the contrary, he gets a real big kick out of the act of butchering someone. If it caused him pain or he didn't like committing this act, he wouldn't do it. Some might call my answer "simplistic" but I don't think it needs to get any more complicated than that. Time and energy spent trying to figure out these individuals is better spent figuring out how to defend yourself against them.

In the end, you really only need to remember one thing about these people; remember that you cannot negotiate or reason with them. If you find yourself in the unfortunate position of being directly confronted by one of these folks, do yourself a favor and save your breath, because you probably don't have many breaths left. In this situation the words "please don't" will be the most useless words in the English language. You cannot appeal to their better nature; they have no better nature. You cannot plead for mercy, because they possess no such emotion. Pity for another human being is a feeling that they will never have. They are not concerned with how much fear and pain they bring to others; in fact, that is their goal. The more misery they spread around the better. Seeing you shaking with fear is one of the benefits of the job for them. Hearing you scream for pity is music to their ears. They relish the act of hurting or killing you. That's what they came there for and nothing that you say to them will change their minds. Accept the fact that they exist and don't stay awake at night wondering why.

Developing a mind-set:

Step-Three: Once you have accepted the fact that there are bad people in this world, you must further accept the fact that <u>nothing</u> justifies their actions.

"He that is good for making excuses is seldom good for anything else."

Benjamin Franklin

"An excuse is worse and more terrible than a lie; for an excuse is a lie guarded."

Alexander Pope

Recognizing that there are truly evil human beings out there goes hand in hand with a firm conviction on your part that nothing justifies their murderous activities. You must come to believe that there is no

Developing a stay-alive mindset

valid excuse for the things that they have done. Be forewarned that espousing such a belief may serve to set you at odds with certain segments of our society. Modern America is overrun with those who will make endless excuses for the criminals and terrorists among us.

On September 11th the fires in Manhattan and Washington were not yet out when the excuses started to ooze to the surface. The peddlers of this insane view were pretty low key at first, just whispers here and there on the nightly news. They couldn't be too loud early on, or they might have been dragged out of their towers of "hate America first" liberalism and lynched, but as time passed they got louder. Today, almost three years after the fact, you don't have to look very hard to find someone willing to get in your face and try to convince you that that terrible day was actually our fault. Every time a suicide bomber kills a busload of people, someone comes on my television to explain to me how it wasn't the bombers fault or the fault of the organization that recruited and trained him. We even have people out there now trying to tell us what a nice guy Saddam Hussein was and how all those mass graves was just his particular leadership style.

It used to be that the average criminal was held in general contempt. And, in this country, and was felt be directly liable for his actions. When I was growing up, this was a generally held belief, and, to some degree, the media and entertainment industry supported it. In the nightly dramas were good people and bad people, and the bad people had no excuse for their assault against the lives and property of the good people. When the news commentator reported on a crime, it was done with either a totally neutral tone or the commentator portrayed a belief in the inherent wrongness of the act.

Over the last few decades, however, the cultural attitude towards the criminal element in this country has changed and not for the better. A new ideology has come about and it has, to a degree, penetrated every aspect of our society. Central to this new ideology is the idea that the lawbreakers themselves are somehow no longer at fault, and slowly the criminal element in this nation has been relieved of all responsibility for their actions. Instead of pinning the blame for the crime on the perpetrator of the crime, it is now put upon a whole list of phantoms. "Poverty breeds crime" is on of the standard lines put forth in any discussion of this issue. If someone committed a brutal robbery, it was because of the poverty they grew up in and not because of the basis of their nature. The fact that they don't have all the material things that they think they ought to is evidently justification enough to shove a gun or knife in somebody's face and take what they want. A savage sexual assault is now said to have happened because the perpetrator was abused as a child or had a domineering female presence early in his life. Sometimes bloody killing is attributed to the "inner rage" felt by the poor unfortunate murderer who was only responding, after all, to the inequities of this "racist and sexist society." Based on all that, how could you even think of blaming the poor criminal for his crime?

After a couple of decades of this indoctrination against common sense, the crime rate in this country exploded in our faces, and is it any wonder? Murders, rapes, armed robberies, and all other forms of crime skyrocketed out of control. Brain-washed against the very idea of self-defense, tens of thousands of American citizens have fallen dead in this onslaught. Shot, stabbed, beaten, and strangled, the body count has reached epidemic proportions. The graveyards are full and getting fuller by the day. The criminal populace was given a green light and merrily set about creating mayhem, and why shouldn't they? If you were a thug by profession, who would you rather go up against, a population tutored in the art of trendy helplessness, or a bunch of folks who could and would protect themselves?

If you are going to acquire a mindset for self-defense, you are going to have to consciously resist this mass indoctrination. You have to develop the conviction that there is no justification or excuse for a violent criminal act no matter what the circumstances of his or her life. Having developed this attitude, stick with it. Verbally challenge those who would seek to excuse the inexcusable and don't

Developing a stay-alive mindset

be nice about it. The more that average citizens express their outrage at the criminal element, the less power that element will have.

In summary, developing a proper mindset for self-defense will require you to do three things. First, value your existence and take direct personal responsibility for the continuation of that existence. Second, accept the fact that there is actually such a thing as a completely evil human being. Don't waste time trying to figure out why these monsters are here; just understand that they are here and they will hurt you if they can. Third, develop a core belief that nothing justifies the actions of a violent criminal. Once you have accepted these facts and incorporated them into your overall viewpoint on life, all else will follow.

Chapter 5
How to have a fight; facing the actual confrontation;

"Boy, there is no nice way to have a fight, so don't try."

Kit Cessna

"It is fatal to enter any war without the will to win it."

Douglas MacArthur

So far I have covered all the periphery subjects but now the time has come to discuss the main issue. What are you going to do if you are actually faced with this most unpleasant of circumstances, a real attack? "It will never happen to me" is the most commonly held view out there. That view is a basic aspect of human nature and not really grounded in truth. So strong is the desire to live implanted within us that it is almost impossible for the average person to truly visualize themselves in a life or death encounter with another human being. Most people will simply put this possibility out of their mind and refuse to discuss it logically. Again, that is human nature and while it may let you off the hook for a while, that denial attitude will lead you right to your grave if the horrific event ever actually occurs. If this book is to be of any value at all, this subject must be faced and discussed in detail. Realizing right up front that I would not be talking to a military or police audience (as I usually am), I had to think long and hard about what I was going to say on this subject. I decided that while I would be no more graphic or macabre than necessary, I had a moral obligation to talk straight about this matter.

How to have a fight; facing the actual confrontation;

I am fully aware that you and I will probably view this matter from completely different directions. My life story is not a typical one in comparison to the majority of my fellow citizens. From the time that I was a very young child I knew, without a shred of doubt, the path that my life would take. I would be a soldier and an elite one at that. While most kids my age were listening to rock and roll, I was singing "The Ballad of the Green Berets." I couldn't have cared less about what happened on the football field or the basketball court. My boyhood heroes were the men who stormed the beaches of Normandy or flung themselves out of their lumbering transport aircraft the night before in that most epic of events. *Air War over Hitler's Germany* was one of the books that could be found on the small shelf in my room when I was a boy. Even at a young age, I could clearly see in my mind's eye the dramatic scenes of that particular part of that particular conflict. Closing my eyes I could envision those scared teenagers of long ago, their oxygen masks frozen to their faces, as they blasted away at the near-suicidal Luftwaffe pilots who came at them time and time again.

Nor were my early imaginings restricted to the Second World War, as I pored over history book after history book. I could make myself be there with the Legions of Rome as they smashed into the screaming hordes of Barbarians on the border of the Empire. I could hear the crisp bugle calls of the surrounded cavalrymen on the Little Big Horn River as well as see the decimated lines of British infantry standing on a blood-smeared ridgeline outside a small Belgian village called Waterloo.

To be a soldier and to go eventually into harm's way was my calling and I wasn't particularly interested in anything else. "God, what a child to have-I feel sorry for your parents" is the refrain going through some of your minds, I'm sure. "You must have had a death wish or something," others might speculate. Wrong on both counts. During the course of my unusual childhood I never was in serious trouble of any kind. My grades were not enviable, but they were acceptable. There were no incidents of drug usage or shoplifting, no late night visits from the police, no pregnant girlfriends or any of the other pathetic activities so often engaged in by my peers. You would have been lucky to have a kid like me. Nor was it my desire to die an early death, though I simply accepted that this could be my fate as a result of the profession that I was going to choose.

As it turned out, I got my wish and had a full military career. I was fortunate to have had the opportunity to serve in the most elite units that the United States Army has. I got to see the world and, upon occasion, get shot at. I did all the things that I dreamed about as a young boy, and then some. By God's good will, I came out the other end alive with all limbs and brain still attached. Many of my friends were not so lucky, I assure you. My fascination with military history is unabated and, as my wife can attest, the local library gets a visit from me quite often. As I now read about some long-forgotten conflict, I feel sadness at those who had their life cut short and realize that, on at least a few occasions that could have been me. I also feel a warm sense of camaraderie with the people in those pages. Be they a long dead Legionnaire of the Caesar or a blue-clad private at Gettysburg, for now and evermore they are my brothers.

My willingness to go into harm's way did not end with my military career. Upon retirement I was offered a position as an instructor for the U.S. State Department Anti-Terrorist Assistance Program (ATAP). As a result of that job, I came to know many of the middle and high-ranking personnel of the local law enforcement agencies, and they facilitated my entry into their somewhat hazardous profession. I have served both as a uniformed patrol officer and SWAT Team member and am currently act as a training consultant to the Baton Rouge Police Special Response Team. My point in all this is that you and I are more than likely going to view this subject from different angles. A lethal encounter with another human being is something that I have been trained for since I was a teenager, and upon occasion that training has been put to use. I fully realize that your experience with this grim subject is either extremely limited or non-existent. However, there is no reason that you cannot learn to competently defend yourself in a lethal force encounter. You don't have to be a veteran of Delta Force or a long-serving SWAT officer to win in a fight for your life. What you do have to do is face a few facts and make some hard decisions about what you are and are not willing to do in that fight.

For most people reading this part of my book will not be a pleasant experience, as you will have to think about some possibilities that you may rather not think about. You will have to visualize yourself performing an act of extreme violence in defense of your self, an act of violence that could well result in the death of your attacker. Fortunately, unpleasant is not the same as impossible.

The real truth about violence

"There is a violence that liberates, and a violence that enslaves; there is a violence that is moral and a violence that is immoral."

Unknown

Oftentimes in a society there will be commonly held and stated beliefs. These beliefs exist simply because they have been repeated often enough that they have taken on the embodiment of facts. There is no actual proof that these beliefs are true; nevertheless, they exist. It seems that if a saying is repeated often enough, then it is accepted as gospel among a large portion of any given population. We have such beliefs in twenty-first century America and they are repeated over and over. One of these myths has become somewhat ingrained and is an ideology of sorts.

"Violence never solved anything, you know?" We have all heard this sanctimonious and inaccurate statement again and again in our lives. This particular utterance is frequently used in any discussion concerning the right of an individual to defend themselves against a criminal attack. The premise of this statement is that all acts of violence are the same, morally wrong. A violent act committed in defense of oneself is put into the same category as a violent act committed in an unprovoked attack. The self-righteous promulgators of this myth would lump you into the same class as the criminal who caused the encounter to begin with. Woe be unto you, should you have the unremitting gall to actually raise your hand against your murderous attacker! According to the "all violence is wrong" crowd, you have now sunk to the same base level as the person who confronted you with the intent of doing harm. Some of the biggest propagators of this "all violence is wrong" ideology are people in our society who hold positions of authority. Senators and mayors, sheriffs and police chiefs have all raised their voices at one time or another and publicly stated this view. Schoolteachers, clergy, and elected officials have added to the din.

If you are an individual who truly believes that there is no moral difference between an act of violence committed in self defense and an act of violence committed with criminal intent, then I have a few questions for you. If a person finds himself or herself in a situation where they are about to be killed and their only option is to resist the attack, what would you have them do? If the use of violence on their part is inherently wrong and no other defensive options exist (such as fleeing the encounter), are they then required to simply submit to their fate? In other words, are they obligated to die? Should they give up the only life they have in order to not fall from some lofty moral plain? Don't tell me that these things don't happen. They happen all the time, and the proof of their happening is the dead victims that we hear about almost every single day. This is a hard question for the anti-violence crowd, and I haven't heard any of them give a clear answer in my lifetime.

For those in positions of authority, the question is repeated. Are the citizens living in your jurisdiction or district obligated to die for you? Are they obligated to give up their life in order to fit into your theory of what our society should be like? Or is it the simple truth that a person in your position is willing to accept a few casualties so as not to have your views challenged? Again, don't tell me that

How to have a fight; facing the actual confrontation;

this doesn't happen. It has happened time and again. I will never forget watching television during the Los Angeles riots that sprung up in the aftermath of the Rodney King trial. Upon seeing that a significant number of citizens were ready and willing to use lethal force to defend their lives and property, both city government and law enforcement officials unhesitatingly lumped together the rampaging lawbreakers into the same group as the beleaguered citizens.

Like a lot of other commonly held views these days, this idea that all violence is the same is a load of absolute garbage! In the first place, there is a clear moral difference between an act of self-defense and an act of aggression, and this is something that the anti-violence crowd seems unwilling to accept. While the physical actions taken may be the same in both events, they are worlds apart when it comes to the issue of right or wrong. A person who uses violence (even lethal violence) in the course of keeping him or herself alive will never be the same as a person who uses violence in an unprovoked attack. Don't worry about theoretically "sinking down to that level." That will never happen. If you are not a predator now, in all likelihood, you will never be one. You could kill a person a day in legitimate acts of self defense and still be the absolute moral superior to the person who has committed only one unjustified attack.

Remember in chapter four when I talked about assigning your life a value and sticking by that decision? Assigning your life its proper value means that you hold that life to be more valuable than the life of your attacker. That clearly means that if you are attacked, coming out the other end of the situation alive and unharmed is the only option that you are prepared to accept. This is not only morally right; it is you only logical choice in this set of circumstances. Making this choice may mean that you have to use lethal, violent force against your attacker.

The real truth about violence is that it has solved more human issues than any other endeavor. If this were not true, then we would not practice it so much. I know that isn't the popular, politically correct view, yet I maintain that it is true. If a murderer confronts you

Equal Or Greater Force

with the intent and ability to kill you and you use violence to defeat the attack, who can say that violence didn't solve the problem? Who can say that violence didn't solve the problem even if it turned out to be the exact same act as that which was intended by the killer? There is violence that is justified and violence that is not. Violence directed at the perpetrator of a deadly attack on you or your loved ones is inherently justified, no matter what others may have to say about it.

If there had been some lethal violence visited upon the September 11th hijackers before they completed their deadly mission, thousands of our fellow citizens would still be with us. Had these monsters been killed on that fateful morning before they could carry out their tasks, then the United States of America would not have had to go to war. There would have been no Afghanistan, no Iraq, and hundreds of thousands of people would still be alive. In fact, there was some real violence bestowed upon some of those foreign murderers that day, and the result was that they were prevented from carrying out their part of the attack. To whoever feels it necessary to point out to me that all the people who offered violence to their attackers ended up dead, I will point out that the fact that those people would have ended up dead anyway and the proof of that was in what happened to the three flights that proceeded them. On the local scene, if there had been some real violence visited on the Baton Rouge serial killer at some time during his rampage, then there would be some daughters, mothers, and wives still with us today.

It has been said that violence just leads to more violence and in some cases that is true. Every day we can turn on the television and see this happening. The former Yugoslavia, the Gaza Strip, and the situation in Iraq are prime examples of daily savagery that serves only to perpetuate itself. I would maintain, though, that even in the middle of those types of brutal conflicts, there are cases of legitimate self-defense by individuals. In any event, it is ludicrous to compare the non-stop fighting on some foreign shore to an attempt by an American citizen to simply stay alive in the face of an unprovoked criminal attack.

How to have a fight; facing the actual confrontation;

If you are one of those few people who absolutely reject violence, no matter what the circumstances, then this is for you. I'm talking to those people who truly have the conviction to forgo defending themselves with lethal force even if it means their own demise. First, if you really have the courage of your convictions, then you have my respect, but not agreement. Second, you have every right to make that decision for yourself. Third, you have absolutely no right to make that decision for anyone else, so don't.

There is no nice way to have a fight, so don't try. Be willing to inflict a lethal wound on your attacker!

"There is not fifty ways of fighting, there is only one, and that is to win."

Andre Malraux

"In a fight for your life you can be either the winner or the loser; winner is the recommended choice."

Kit Cessna

There is another basic truth about this issue and it would seem to be obvious, but I'm afraid that this truth has escaped many people. There is no nice way to have a fight. No way to make this situation anything other than what it is, a violent encounter between two or more human beings. The two sides seek to do bodily harm to each other, and sometimes death or serious injury is the result. In this situation you have two choices. You can be the winner or you can be the loser. Each choice comes with certain drawbacks and neither one will be pleasant to experience. The consequences of being the winner will be discussed in a further chapter. For now we will concentrate on the consequences of being the loser.

The consequence for being the loser in a fight against a murderous attacker is almost all bad. You will at the very least suffer grievous bodily injury and may end up in a brain-damaged, catatonic state for the rest of your life. More than likely, though, in an attack of this sort you will suffer death. That's right, death; as in stone cold, slab lying, toe tagged, in a drawer in the morgue under the tender care of some yawning city employee, never to breath again, totally, completely, irrevocably dead! You will be the headline of the next morning's newspaper as the media spews the details of your brutal death out to the public at large. You will now be a statistic added to the long list of crime victims in this country and you won't know a thing about it. No more todays, no more tomorrows, all yesterdays from that point forward. And the best part of the deal is this: your death was probably not peaceful or painless. No, you will have gone through pure hell just to get to the point of being no longer alive. You will have been shot, stabbed, beaten, raped, or a combination thereof.

If you are fortunate, your killing did not take an unreasonable length of time to accomplish. Maybe it was over within a few seconds, a few minutes, or an hour or two. If you are not the sort who is good at picking lottery numbers, maybe you didn't get off so easily. Maybe you were one of the lucky few that got held onto and played with for a while. Perhaps you were tied up in some abandoned structure, lying on a cold dirt floor, shivering and shaking from the cold and the pain of wounds already suffered. Maybe you lay there for days wondering how long it would take for him to come back and start playtime again, knowing full well that no matter how long it was, he would be back.

I said that being a dead loser is almost all bad, but there is actually one good point to this outcome. You will not be around to see the aftermath of your homicide. You will not have to view the crime scene when your decomposed corpse is dragged out of some hole in the ground or out of some swamp. You will not have to behold

How to have a fight; facing the actual confrontation;

the shredded pile of rotten bone and meat that is left after the forces of nature have had a few weeks or months to go about their tasks. You will not have to see even the veteran homicide investigators turn away from the unrecognizable remains that were once you. You will not witness the horrified shock on the face of you family and friends as the police inform them of your fate. You will not have to witness the next few days, weeks, or months as they struggle to come to grips with what has happened to you. You will not even be there years later to see the sad reflection on their faces when it is your birthday or Christmas Eve. Best of all, you will not be there to see them eventually put your memory away deep inside themselves and get on with their lives without you. Sound grim? Well, it's a grim subject and any attempt on my part to make it nicer would be dishonest.

So what's the answer? It is pretty simple, actually. If you find yourself in a fight for your life, you do just that, fight! Forget about being nice, and fight your way to survival. Use any means at your disposal and put out of your mind any concern with the physical well being of your opponent. Hurt your attacker as badly as you can and that includes killing him, if it comes to that. Yes, that's right, I said kill him if that's what it takes to make him stop coming. Believe me, he is going to quickly lose interest in hurting you if he is dealing with a catastrophic injury to himself.

I have read about or heard about case after case wherein the victim fought back but unfortunately didn't prevent their attacker from doing what he came there to do. The ones that survived tearfully maintain, "I fought back but it didn't work." Obviously, most of the victims that I am talking about are women and my heart goes out to them. However, an expression of sympathy for these unfortunate women doesn't change the circumstances of what happened to them. The brutal truth about these situations is that the victim either didn't fight hard enough or fought ineffectively. Pushing, shoving, and squirming away don't cut it in this type of encounter. You need to pay very close attention to these next few paragraphs because they are the central point that I am trying to make in this book.

Equal Or Greater Force

Surviving a fight for your very existence will more than likely mean having to inflict some real physical harm on your attacker, and I mean real harm. I am convinced that the average female in this society (and a few of the males) is completely clueless when it comes to the definition of inflicting harm. They simply have no idea of the extreme level of injury that I am talking about. Most women are also totally unaware of the level of pain and injury that a male body can take and keep right on coming. As the owner of an aging model, I can attest to this fact. During my lifetime I have been shot through the hand, had broken bones and ligaments, and suffered severe lacerations accompanied by alarming blood loss. In all of theses circumstances I was, for a short time, able to continue what I was doing when the injury happened. Am I some sort of Superman? No, I am far from that. Ingrained within my psychological make-up is the ability to temporarily ignore pain and continue. Most adult males have this capability to some degree or another. I am not for a minute saying that your attacker will not feel pain when you sink your fingernails into his flesh. Pain will most definitely be felt; it just may not have the desired effect.

Fighting effectively means that you are able to inflict such a level of injury on your opponent that he is no longer physically capable of continuing the battle. It may mean a major bone injury that will not allow him to get to back on his feet or grasp an object with his hands. It may also come about as a result of blunt trauma to the head that will result in unconsciousness. This may also mean severe blood loss accompanied by shock and incapacitation that comes from being shot in a vital body part. Surviving such an encounter may mean having to do some really bad things to another human being. If you are going to be effective when the time comes, you are going to have to think about it beforehand. You are going to have to visualize yourself performing the act. If your weapon is something like a baseball bat, you may have to hit your attacker repeatedly before he goes down (see Chapter 6 for the lowdown on ball bats.) I don't mean just whacking him a few times; I mean really hitting him again and again until he is no longer a threat.

How to have a fight; facing the actual confrontation;

If you are fortunate enough to possess a firearm and are willing and able to use it, realize that you may have to shoot your opponent more than once and may have to literally empty the weapon into his body. In a face-to-face encounter with a vicious killer, you may have to injure him to the point that he is dead, period. Being willing to do grievous bodily harm to another human being is key to your ability to win in a fight for your life. If you are the one still standing after it is all over, not having been raped and/or murdered, then you will know that you have fought effectively. If you are going to have any chance at all, you have to make the decision that you will use deadly force if you have to. That's the truth of the matter, and all else is immaterial.

Now you might think that being willing to do whatever it takes to stay alive in these circumstances would be a commonly held viewpoint, a "no brainer" so to speak. I mean the guy is trying to kill you, isn't he? So what's the problem here? Still, I am amazed at the number of people that I have heard voice some inherent unwillingness to hurt someone even if that person is in the very act of hurting them. I will admit that a person of my background finds this attitude puzzling. I am convinced, however, that this stated conviction is more an indication of the individual in question being unwilling to think about the situation than it is an indication of an inability to perform the act. Some things are unpleasant to contemplate and this is certainly one of them. Most people don't sit around thinking about what it would feel like to kill another person. They may watch it on television or the movies, but that is a scene far removed from the reality of their life.

Using deadly force against another human being is not going to be a pleasant experience regardless of how justified your actions are. It is not a nice thing to witness and it is even worse to do. It is not something that is enjoyed by a person with any sort of normal value system. It is, however, something that you may have to do and if you have not made the decision to defend yourself in the face of an attack, you should think about it before the event. Make your decision now, not during the event. A fight with a serial killer in a darkened hallway is not the time or place to examine your core values. Keep one important fact in mind. Your attacker has already made his decision on this issue, and he will stick by that decision. The average run-of-the mill serial killer does not creep down your hallway at three in the morning wrestling with a moral dilemma. He came there to hurt you and, if you let him, that is exactly what he will do. He has made up his mind on the issue, and you should do the same.

When we talk about defending ourselves with lethal force in a situation such as this we are, in most cases, talking about using a gun. Unless you are some sort of martial arts master or a world-class knife fighter, then a firearm is the most logical choice, and that is what is used in the overwhelming majority of self-defense cases. So we are talking about discharging a firearm into another human body, probably at close range. Having seen it done, done it, and having had it done to me, I can assure you that it is very unpleasant. Hollywood may be able to pretty it up and put a heroic face on this act but the reality is much different. I do not speak from just theory and have myself been on the receiving end of a bullet. The incident occurred during a SWAT operation against a hostage taker in Baton Rouge, Louisiana. During the resolution of that incident, I was unfortunate enough to get shot through the hand by the suspect. Not exactly the stuff of a Rambo movie, I know, but the criminal was real, the bullet was real, and, most of all, my hand was real.

The shock and impact of that little piece of lead traveling at several hundred feet a second was incredible, and you would have to feel it to believe it. It knocked the stuffing out of me, and that was just in the hand and not through the chest cavity, or some other vital area. If you have to shoot someone, it is going to hurt him and hurt him bad. If he is not killed outright, then he is going to go through some real trauma and pain. A gun is designed with one purpose in mind and that is to inflict a lethal injury on the person that it hits. There is no way around that fact.

How to have a fight; facing the actual confrontation;

To those of you who think that you are, for one reason or another, incapable of performing this act, I say this. There hasn't been a human being born who cannot kill someone. Everybody has the capability whether they want to believe it or not. I'm going to use a hypothetical situation to prove my point. I want you to visualize yourself in this situation and think about what you would be feeling. First, I take you to a firing range and have you shoot several hundred bullets through a small caliber revolver. I let you blast away until both you and I are satisfied that you are completely familiar with the operation of that weapon. After our range practice session, I then take you to a location that is equipped with a swimming pool. I have you enter the deep end of the pool and hang onto the edge while I prepare you for the exercise. I will then have my assistants enter the pool and tie your feet together. They will attach a heavy weight to your feet with a length of chain that will only allow your head to be barely above the surface. They will then handcuff your left hand to the side of the pool, which will severely limit your ability to move around on the surface. I will place a scuba diver's mask on your face so that you will be able to clearly see me while you are under water. In your right hand I will tape that same revolver loaded with hollow point ammunition, guaranteed to be really nasty in its effect at close range. Now you have a gun in your hand that you cannot get rid of. I will then give you the following instructions; "I'm going to kneel down, get a good grip on your hair and hold your head under water now, and I will not let go until you make me." I grant you a few seconds to contemplate this statement and then under you go. Sometime in the next thirty seconds to one minute you will put that gun in my face and pull the trigger, I guarantee it. You will use that gun to get me to let go of you. If by chance you are some sort of Olympic class swimmer or you like to spend your leisure hours free diving into the murky depths, we might be there for a little while longer, but the end is going to be the same. When you get your head back above water, you will not be thinking about the fact that you just killed or gravely injured someone. You will only be thinking about how good it feels to breathe again. Only after your heart rate and respiration have returned to normal, and you have been released from the situation, will you contemplate the results of your actions.

Now obviously you and I are not going to visit the YMCA anytime soon and I would never place someone in this situation. However, every single one of you knows what it feels like to be on the verge of drowning. You also know that, at that moment, you will do whatever it takes to escape that fate. My point on the matter is simple: in those circumstances you would have pulled the trigger. You would not have shot me because you are a cold-hearted killer. You would not have shot me because you didn't like me or because you are a bad person. You would have shot me because you didn't want to die. You would have realized that shooting me was the only option, and you would have killed me to stay alive. If I any other person were crazy enough to actually conduct that experiment, you would be justified in the killing.

Digest that scenario for a few minutes and then answer this question. What is the difference between what I was doing to you in that hypothetical swimming pool and what some murderer is going to do to you in reality? As I see it, the only difference is that in my scenario, you were confronted with the irrefutable fact of your impending death at my hands. In a confrontation with a murderer, this fact may not be immediately apparent until it is too late. The only other difference that I see is that death by drowning may be a little easier than whatever the local Hannibal Lector has planned for you. Don't try and tell me that you cannot kill someone. If you find yourself in the right set of circumstances, you can and will.

Do count yourself the loser before the event; plan on winning the fight.

"Believe you are defeated, believe it long enough, and it is likely to become a fact."

Norman Vincent Peale

"They can conquer who believe they can."

Vergil

Winning a fight comes down to a few simple items. You have to take the appropriate defensive action and keep your fear under control. Central to this is a firm conviction on your part that you can win and survive. No one can foresee the future, and your murder is not a foregone conclusion. There is no rulebook that maintains that you have to lose the encounter, and there will never be such a rulebook unless you write it beforehand. If you decide that you are going to prevail in this confrontation, you might just do that. If you decide before the event that you will lose the encounter, then you probably will. This defeatist mindset is clearly illustrated in the often-heard comment by some women when the subject of gun ownership for self-defense is brought up. "He will just take it away from me," is the usual response. Well ladies, he will if you let him. I cannot guarantee that you will never find yourself in such a close quarter encounter that this possibility will arise. Yes that situation could in fact happen, but don't make the decision beforehand that your attacker will win. I'm going to let you in a little secret on this subject.

Every police officer that spends any amount of time on the mean streets thinks about this possibility every time he or she goes out there. That's right; they are just as concerned about getting relieved of their weapon, as an untrained civilian would be because the threat is there and it could happen. This possibility doesn't keep them from doing their jobs and it shouldn't keep you from being willing to defend yourself. While I was in the process of writing this book, a Baton Rouge police officer was shot and killed with her own gun while attempting to apprehend a shoplifting suspect at a local Wal-Mart. Terrible as that incident was, it didn't stop the other officers from going to work the next day. Besides, if your attacker is that close and is trying to take your weapon away, shoot him with it, and there is a really good chance that he will let go.

Control your fear or it will get you killed.

"Courage is resistance to fear, mastery of fear—not absence of fear."

Mark Twain

"Present fears are less than horrible imaginings."

William Shakespeare (*Macbeth*)

In a fight for your life, you will have to contend with the emotion of fear. You will have to keep that feeling under control if you are to have a chance of winning. You also must be able to keep this basic emotion restrained during the time leading up to the encounter. This is one of those things that are easier said than done, as fear is one of the most powerful emotions that a human has. If you fail to master your fear, it will master you and it will turn into panic. Panic will rob you of your ability to act coherently, and in the situation of a face-off with a murderer, it will probably get you killed. So you must learn to control this most difficult of emotions, and the best way to learn to control this emotion is to understand it.

In our modern society the emotion of fear has a somewhat bad reputation. Of all the emotions in the human inventory, it is one of the least liked and for good reason. To feel afraid is one of the more unpleasant sensations that we will experience. I'm not taking about the momentary thrill that you get from a carnival ride or the tingle caused by a scary movie. I'm not even talking about the sensations experienced and raved about by the thrill seekers in our culture as they dangle off of thousand-foot-high cliffs or back flip out of an airplane or off a bridge with a bungee cord wrapped around them. Those feelings are just that—thrills. People who participate in those activities have a little secret that they keep to themselves: the gear that they are using will, in all likelihood, keep them from harm. The actual risk to life and limb presented by these behaviors is really no more than you face every day driving to work through heavy rush-hour traffic. Ask yourself this question: how many times in your life have you heard about someone dying in a skydiving accident? Now compare that sum with the number of times that you have heard about someone dying in a traffic accident. If most of the people engaging in those activities actually believed that their death could be a result, they wouldn't be doing them.

The fear that I am talking about is the real deal, genuine heart-pounding terror. The kind of fear that makes your whole body ache and your mouth taste like you've been sucking on an old copper penny. This is the feeling that only happens when you realize that you are going to get seriously hurt or dead. This is the feeling experienced by a person trapped in a burning building who realizes that there is no way out. It is also felt during a lethal close encounter with another human being who is bent on killing you and has the will and the means to do just that. You come to the realization that there is a good chance that you will be leaking your blood into your shag carpet in the next few seconds, because you are going to get shot or receive a knife blade in the abdomen. This guy is going to hurt you and hurt you bad and you are not going to stop him short of some extreme action on your part. Nobody in his or her right mind would claim to enjoy that sensation, but it is just that emotion that you must learn to control if you are going to survive.

Believe it or not, in an extreme situation, fear can be the best friend that you will ever have. Keep it under control, and it can keep you alive and functioning. Mother Nature doesn't make mistakes, and this emotion is in us for a reason. It is our early warning system and part of our combat control center, so to speak. The sensations that you feel are a result of your body making preparations to deal with the situation you are in. It is important to understand those sensations and what they mean.

How the emotion of fear works

During the course of your daily activities, your body is functioning with the parasympathetic nervous system. This basically means that some of your bodily functions are involuntary, just as others are voluntary. Your system is going through its usual activities, including respiration, circulation, digestion, and voluntary muscle movement. Your heart is beating at whatever speed is normal for you and your breathing is regular and unlabored. Your vision is clear and you are concentrating on whatever it is that you are doing. Any excess muscle movement and exertion is voluntary on your part. Everything is normal and you are not feeling any extreme stress or fear. Getting chewed out by your boss or contemplating your financial or marital future doesn't count as stress in this situation.

At the first sign of danger, assuming that you are both lucky enough to get a warning and alert enough to recognize it for what it is, several things will begin to happen. I'm not talking about a direct confrontation yet; I'm talking about the circumstances leading up to that point. For example, you come out into a dark and deserted parking lot late at night and realize that you are all alone. Another example would be to hear an unidentified noise in your house in the wee dark hours. The danger is not here yet, but you are beginning to realize the potential of the situation. At this point you will begin to look around you and try to identify any hazards. You will start moving faster and seek a safe zone, be it your automobile or some other place of security. Your heart rate is somewhat elevated and your breathing will come more rapidly, which will allow for a more rapid physical reaction to the actual identification of a threat. These are all simply the symptoms of your fear waking up and getting on the job of keeping you alive.

When the lethal threat is positively identified and the reality of the situation dawns on you is the moment of truth. You are now face to face with the monster, and there is no getting away. Your body immediately switches over to the sympathetic nervous system wherein most of your physiological reactions are no longer voluntary. This is sometimes referred to as the "fight or flight reaction" when the body is getting ready to do either. The main sensation that you will feel is the rush of adrenaline into your blood stream, and it is called a rush because that is actually what is. It can be described as the feeling of some internal impact on your body as this chemical shoots through your system. This occurrence will cause a number of other events in your body. Blood will be drained away from the extremities and the surface of the body so that the internal organs will receive a better supply. Your heart rate will radically elevate and your breathing will become more shallow and rapid. You may also experience what is referred to as "tunnel vision." This is the concentration of your vision directly at the threat, and you can lose some of your peripheral vision as a result. In this condition you are actually able to run faster and fight harder than normal although you may perceive that just the opposite is true. The main thing to remember about these systems and feelings is that it is okay to have them. In fact, you have no choice in the matter and you will experience them whether you want to or not. These feelings are not your enemy. Although they are unpleasant to experience, these reactions can keep you alive and allow you to either win the fight or successfully flee.

Now it is time to answer the million-dollar question: how do I keep my fear under control and make it work for me instead of against me? Unfortunately, there is no single simple answer to this inquiry. People are not the same, and each individual will feel things differently. No two individuals will feel the same level of fear in the same situation. This difference in perception is a result of a number of factors including physical condition, health, previous experience and training, and above all, mind set. This is not a new subject in the story of humanity, because countless human beings have dealt with this level of fear and dealt with it successfully.

Every soldier who goes into battle for the first time has gone through this situation, and no group has dealt more extensively with this subject than the military and in particular the combat organizations within that structure. Being able to operate under conditions of extreme fear and stress is inherent to a soldier's ability to accomplish the mission. In an organization such as Delta Force, the ability of the individual to control his fear is placed into the same category as the ability to use a weapon. Not only is the individual required to keep this emotion under complete control, he is expected to be able to perform complicated tasks at the same time. A special operations soldier would be unable to function at all were he not able to continually subdue his fear. The necessity on the part of the individual to keep his emotions under control is not restricted to those who engage in ground operations. An F-16 pilot could not fly his aircraft through a swarm of missiles and tracers over Baghdad without being able to control and conquer fear. The law enforcement community has its own experiences with this issue, and thousands of cops have faced a deadly confrontation and lived to tell about it. All of these people have to one degree or another learned to keep their fear under control during moments of extreme stress, and so can you.

Most soldiers and police officers secretly enjoy entertaining a civilian audience with great stories of personal daring and courage. During such a recounting any display of humility or modesty on their part is just an act, believe me. I don't claim to be any different and I would like nothing better than to spend the rest of this chapter describing all my life's adventures. I have felt extreme fear many times in my life and successfully conquered that emotion to one degree or another. As gratifying as it would be for me to recount all my experiences, it would be somewhat pointless in light of the overall message of this book. You and I are more than likely viewing this issue from a different base of experience. There are a couple of things that I have learned over the years, however, that I can pass on to you directly.

Develop a sense of anger at those who would harm you. Anger can control fear.

"Neutral men are the devil's allies."

Edwin Hubbel Chaplin

"Neutrality, as a lasting principle, is an evidence of weakness."

Lajos Kossuth

As human beings, we are equipped with an entire range of emotional responses, and fear is one of the strongest sentiments that we can feel in a given situation. Other emotions can be somewhat difficult to display for the average person, but fear is easy to produce. There is one other emotion, however, that can be at least as powerful, if not more so. In fact, this is the only emotion in the human inventories that can actually override and conquer fear. The best part of this emotion is that it is easy for the average person to display.

Anger is the one emotion that can overcome your feelings of terror. It is the single feeling that will conquer all others. I'm not talking about going crazy and flying into an uncontrolled, maniacal rage. No, I'm talking about a controlled but inflamed emotional state. If you get mad enough, your fear will start to take a back seat. Anger will also give you an aggressive countenance that you may not ordinarily be able to project. An appropriate level of controlled anger can goad you into taking action that will save your life.

Like fear, anger gets a bad review these days; it's as if this basic emotion has been declared illegal. All across the land hundreds attend anger management classes (either voluntarily or as part of a deferred sentence). Once again society has made some sort of blanket manifesto that deems all feelings of this sort to be the indicator of some kind of mental trouble. All anger is bad just like all violence is bad, the theory goes. It seems that common sense has been taken out of the equation. I say that some anger is justified and some is not. Displaying an uncontrolled rage when someone inadvertently cuts you off in traffic is obviously not called for. On the other hand, when you are confronted with a killer, anger may be just what you need to stay alive.

The good part is that you don't even have to wait until you are confronted with a lethal threat to start developing this feeling of controlled rage. You are fully justified in having these feelings. Picking up the morning paper and reading about yet another savage attack should do the trick. Indeed, hearing about a criminal attack should make us all mad. So rather that walking around scared to death of these creeps, start walking around feeling angry with them. You will be amazed at how different the world looks once this becomes your attitude.

How to have a fight; facing the actual confrontation;

Remember that you have a responsibility to yourself and your loved ones to stay alive.

"To succeed in keeping alive against odds, to live after an event that has threatened a person."

Webster's Dictionary

Definition of the word "survive"

"Whatever it takes, make sure that you are one of the ones still breathing when it's over."

Kit Cessna

For the soldier and the cop, prevailing in a lethal encounter is about more than simple survival. That is certainly one of their goals, but it may not be the overriding factor. They may not have the option of just coming out of the encounter alive. A soldier in combat has the duty to seek out a confrontation with the enemy even if the odds are against him. Being alive at the end of the battle, while certainly desirable for him (and, believe it or not, his commanders) may not be possible. For the soldier, success will be judged based on whether or not he accomplished his mission in the given circumstances. He can fail to survive the encounter and still be judged to have been successful. In wartime, a soldier literally has a duty to show bravery in a lethal confrontation. The laws that govern military service back up this duty, and failing to show a proper amount of physical courage can have dire results. In February 1945, U.S. Army Private Edward (Eddie) Slovik was blindfolded and tied to a pole in the yard of a German farmhouse located in the Ardennes. On the command of an officer, Slovik's fellow American soldiers shot him to death for the distinctly military crime of desertion. All of the regulations that allowed for that execution are still in place today.

A police officer who fails to perform adequately in a lethal confrontation will probably not find himself facing a firing squad made up of his fellow officers. There is no Manual for Courts Martial in the world of law enforcement. However, failing to show a proper amount of courage and resolve in a life and death situation can still have severe consequences for the cop. He can be brought up on criminal charges and/or face harsh disciplinary actions from his department. Even if he escapes the wrath of his agency, he may be held responsible for the death of other officers (or civilians) as a result of his actions or inactions. Finally, he may be subjected to a level of contempt and derision from his fellow officers that will not allow his career to continue. Like the soldier, the police officer has a legal obligation to confront danger and can fail to survive the encounter and still be deemed successful in his efforts.

As an ordinary citizen you have no such obligations, nor should you. Unlike the soldier or the cop, you are not required to confront anyone and you have the inherent right to avoid any such situation if you can. Should you choose to flee a lethal encounter, that decision cannot and will not be held against you. Somebody may try to second-guess your actions at a later date, but that is about as far as things will go. I would submit, however, that you have some obligations in this matter and these responsibilities are more of a moral nature than a legal one. It is my contention that you have an obligation to survive a lethal encounter for the benefit of both yourself and those who are close to you. Your husband or wife has a right to expect you to use every means possible to stay alive and your children have this same right. Those that you brought into this world have the right to your presence while they are growing up. All those close to you have the right to expect you to do your utmost to survive a lethal confrontation with another human being. This obligation includes those beyond your immediate family, especially if you are someone whom others have come to count on as part of their daily life. If you were to suddenly desert those around you for strictly personal reasons, you would be rightly criticized. Abandoning those same people because you failed to do your best against an attacker deserves some of the same criticism, in my opinion. If that sounds harsh, remember that is isn't nearly as harsh as what your killer has planned for you.

Whatever happens, do not quit.

"Do not go gentle into that good night. Rage, rage against the dying of the light."

Dylan Thomas

"It's never over until it's over." When I was younger I used to think that was just a quaint saying, but now I know that it is true. In the context of this subject, its meaning is simple. The fight isn't over until it is really over. Don't count yourself out; that's somebody else's job. If you find yourself in a situation where you are fighting for your very survival, then you don't stop for anything while you are still alive and moving. Plenty of people have received grievous injuries and have gone on living. Plenty of people have gone into a fight, and the odds appeared to be completely against them, yet they prevailed in the end. Many people have been in a situation where they thought that they were dead, only to live to tell about it. If this unfortunate event occurs in your life, make sure you live to tell about it. Whatever you do, don't quit!

Make physical preparations to deal with a lethal encounter.

The military and the law enforcement communities have the task of training their personnel to be able to control fear and take appropriate actions during stressful situations. One of the primary ways that they accomplish this task is with training. These instructions are ongoing and, for the most part, conducted during times when there is no current threat. The average soldier spends only a fraction of his career in actual combat, and the average police officer seldom walks in on a bank robbery. Far more time is spent training for a stressful event than is spent in dealing with one.

Military and police agencies have a distinct advantage in this matter as they have two things going for them, money and time. Those entities have the ability (actually a duty) to focus financial resources and personnel hours on this subject. In the modern military, the infantry soldiers will have, at a minimum, undergone weeks of high intensity training before they actually see combat. In most cases this training will have actually gone on for years. In the law enforcement world, this training may look a little different but can be just as lengthy and focused. Many different subjects are presented during this training. For the soldier, the instruction focuses mainly around the ability to close with and destroy an enemy force. For the police officer, it focuses on the ability to confront a criminal and uphold the law. In both professions, when the time comes to actually face a threat, be it a pre-planned or unexpected encounter, the individual's prior training will dictate how well he or she does in that situation. If the training has been unrealistic and infrequent, then there is a reasonable chance that the individual will lose the encounter. Conversely, if the training is based on reality and administered often enough, then there is a reasonable chance to survive and prevail.

How to have a fight; facing the actual confrontation;

Training a person to survive and prevail in a lethal confrontation is a subject that we could discuss indefinitely. Countless books and instruction manuals have been produced about this subject and indeed individual careers in both fields are totally dedicated to this matter. The possible variations are endless but the military and police train their personnel to do two things. First, recognize a potentially lethal situation before it is too late, and second, react competently to that situation. Although a lot of money and time will be spent, it really gets no more complicated than that.

On the domestic side of the issue, the average person in this society has neither the money nor the time to put a lot of emphasis on training for a confrontation. Even if they did have the same opportunities as the military or police to practice these skills, it is doubtful that many would. Most people would not be interested and even if they were, life has a habit of getting in the way of extra-curricular activities. In any event, it really isn't necessary for you to have the same level or intensity of training as those who serve us in uniform. As a civilian you have a distinct advantage in this arena because your responsibilities are limited. You have to learn only enough to make a competent defensive action and don't have to worry about making an offensive or preemptive action. In any confrontation, the natural advantage goes to the defender.

Being the defender, one of the most important decisions that you will make in preparation for that defense is to decide on how you will go about it. That leads us to the subject of weapons, and that subject will be covered in the next chapter.

Chapter 6
The weapons in the arsenal

"When force is necessary, it must be applied boldly, decisively and completely."

Leon Trotsky

Russian revolutionary 1879-1940

"Put your trust in God, my boys, and keep your powder dry."

Oliver Cromwell

English politician and leader 1599-1658

Having made the decision that you are willing to fight to defend your life, the next step is to decide what tools to use. There is a bit more depth to this subject than you might think, and there are some things that you must take into consideration before you ever put a weapon in your hands. As I stated in Chapter four, your mental outlook, i.e., mindset, will be the determining factor in any confrontation, regardless of your choice of weapons. No weapon is perfect and none of them are guaranteed to get you out of every single situation, despite what Hollywood would have you believe. The best weapon that you have when it comes to defending yourself from an attacker is your ability to think.

<u>Think!</u> Be aware of your surroundings at all times and don't doze through the day

A critical factor in winning or avoiding a fight is to recognize a potentially lethal situation before that situation overtakes you. You will perform much differently in a situation that you clearly understand to be a lethal threat than you will in a situation that you either don't recognize or that you have underestimated. In the swimming pool scenario you would have acted as you did partly because I made my intentions clear to you and proceeded to act upon those intentions. You had some warning of what I was going to do even if it was only a few seconds, and somewhere in the following thirty seconds to one minute, you decided to believe me. In addition to your recognition of my intentions, there was your recognition of the physiological signs that you were getting ready to die. If I hadn't done that, and instead had lured you into that pool on some legitimate pretext, you might not have realized the gravity of the situation until it was too late and you had passed out prior to drowning. <u>When faced with a murderer, denial of reality can and will get you killed.</u>

Recognizing a potentially dangerous situation can be easy or it can be extremely difficult, depending on the circumstances. Someone kicking in your door at three o'clock in the morning is a situation that presents some obvious danger. Crossing a darkened parking garage or spotting someone tailing you falls into the same category. On the other hand, a friendly looking gentleman knocking on your door in the middle of the day may not be as easy to recognize. An appeal for help by a complete stranger on a roadside or a tearful request to use your cell phone is just as difficult to interpret. Keep in mind that all of the aforementioned situations could very well be precursors to a murderous attack. The basic rule for survival dictates that you treat every encounter with caution until you determine otherwise. Women are the overwhelming majority of the victims in these types of attacks and that's because they have a perception problem. The average female in this society is far more trusting of her environment than is good for her. It is as if most women have some sort of mental block that will not allow them to be suspicious of their surroundings.

There is probably not a woman in the world who at one time or another hasn't gotten angry at the significant man in her life because of his visual attraction to other women. Even if he has the self-control to not be obvious about it, you can feel his eyes moving. This reaction to a visual stimulation tends to anger most women, and I suppose in many circumstances that anger is justified. What many women fail to realize, however, is the degree that men are attracted visually to the opposite sex. An attractive woman passing by presents a lure to the average man that is almost impossible to ignore. The amount of discipline that it would take to avoid looking is tremendous and, in fact, fairly rare. Even if the man is capable of showing that level of control, it is usually obvious that he is thinking unclean thoughts. This activity is likely to occur even if the man in question is in a happy, committed relationship. I'm not going to offer an apology for this inherently male trait. This is the way that God made us and I have to think that he had his reasons. Besides, you ladies have a similar weakness.

Instead of being visually vulnerable to a stimulus, women are highly prone to being verbally manipulated. It seems like all some guys have to do is tell them what they want to hear and they are bought and paid for, so to speak. When the Baton Rouge serial killer was finally caught it was, quite naturally, the talk of the town. Baton Rouge is a relatively small southern city, and it was not hard to find people who knew the killer. As the days passed after the arrest, I heard of woman after woman expressing a disbelief that the right man was in custody. Most of these women either knew the offender personally or had had encounters with him in the past. To a person, they all maintained that "he couldn't have committed those terrible crimes, he was a nice guy." The news that this individual had been linked by DNA evidence to at least five killings didn't seem to be all that important.

A few years ago, an incident occurred in yet another city that was suffered the attentions of a serial murder. In this situation, the killings had been going on for close to ten months. The majority of women in the town and surrounding area were by this time living in a perpetual state of fear. The city itself was rather small and was surrounded by dozens of suburbs and private residences. Many of these homes sat on large pieces of property and were not visible from the main highway running through the town. One afternoon a middle-aged woman living in one of these dwellings received an unexpected visitor. A well-dressed, well-spoken black man rang her doorbell and, when she answered, he began a conversation with her. At this point she had the front door open and was talking to him from behind a locked screen door. Her caller was impressed, it seemed, with the color and quality of the curtains hanging in her front window. He went on to tell her how he drove by every day and couldn't get over how well those drapes looked. The woman was evidently so taken in and flattered by the compliment that she completely forgot the fact that the house was not visible from the main road. Even if her visitor had driven by every day, as he claimed, all he would have seen was trees. Continuing his flattery, the man went on to tell the woman how he wanted to persuade his wife to purchase the same style of curtain for their house. He then asked her if he could come inside so he could get a closer look at the curtains and "see if they will fit in my place." The woman was in the act of opening the door when her husband showed up. He had been in the back of the house and had heard his wife talking to someone. As soon as the visitor saw the husband, he broke off the conversation and quickly departed the residence. Imagine the woman's surprise several weeks later when the serial killer was caught and she recognized the curtain lover's face on the television.

These women had made a judgment solely on the killer's demeanor, and no other factor was taken into account. That, ladies, is a deadly weakness. Judging a person's character strictly on how they present themselves can be lethal when facing a potential killer. The bottom line on this issue is simple. Both sexes have their particular weakness when it comes to the subject of the opposite gender. While a man's weakness could serve to get him in trouble with his wife, a woman's weakness could well serve to put her in a graveyard. Ladies, please learn that just because somebody acts nice doesn't mean that he is nice.

Think! **Be ready to defend yourself, but don't provoke a confrontation that you are not prepared to deal with.**

Another weapon that you have in your arsenal is the willingness to avoid the situation altogether. In other words, don't look for trouble. Unlike the soldier or police officer, you have no obligation to initiate action or to seek a confrontation. As a civilian your responsibilities in these types of situations are limited. The only real obligation that you have is to protect those who need protecting and to survive the encounter. I will expand on this a bit, as this is an area that gets a lot of people in trouble. Having a general philosophy of not looking for trouble makes obvious sense and if more people had that outlook, the world would be a better place. Certainly there are a great many people in our society who do live by this rule and, just as certainly, there are people out there who think they do but don't. Avoiding the fight can be a simple matter or it can be complicated one.

Not approaching an area where trouble seems likely is a fairly simple procedure, and all of us have done it from time to time. A darkened alley in a high-crime area is a place that you would not normally venture into. Nor would you routinely move in the direction of an ongoing confrontation especially if it appeared to be getting violent. Driving up to the local branch of your bank and finding it surrounded by police cars is another example of a state of affairs that you might shy away from. These are common sense reactions to a potentially dangerous situation and people do it every day. This is the simple side of the equation and the rules are basic. Unfortunately, there is a more complicated side of this issue and here is where some folks get into trouble. I'm talking about a situation where people either seek out a confrontation or do not avoid one when they should. I'm going to pick on both men and women on this one.

The weapons in the arsenal

In the case of men, the situation that I'm describing usually occurs in response to some real or imagined insult. Someone cuts you off in traffic (either by mistake or deliberately) and here you go on a search and destroy mission. The offender is treated to a barrage of verbal abuse accompanied by single digit gestures. Sometimes a vehicular pursuit ensues as you try to seek vengeance for this colossal affront to your dignity. You will run him to ground, by God, and when you catch up to him there will be hell to pay! Who does this moron think he is? Doesn't this person understand that you are the only person on the road that matters and innocent mistakes are not to be tolerated? You have no idea who you are tangling with, but what does that matter? The only thing that is important is your rage of the moment, and that emotion must be satisfied at any price.

If this is you, the problems are obvious, aren't they? A situation such as this could blow up in your face in a second. When you get into one of these little scraps, you have no idea who you are messing with. Sure, you could be screaming at somebody who is easily intimidated. You could also be howling at a member of the Colombian drug cartel or an Al Qaeda operative. One second you are pouring forth your righteous anger and the next you are in a fight for your life against someone who has a much better chance of winning than you do. It doesn't even have to be someone on the extreme end of the threat scale to be a deadly encounter. It could just be some guy whose tether to reality and morality is getting ready to break anyway. Some borderline psychopath who just needs that one little push to send him over the edge; and here you come.

For the ladies, problems in this area usually arise on the domestic front. A woman is involved in a relationship that has turned violent, and the scenario goes something like this. He has beaten you before so there is no doubt in your mind that he will resort to such measures again. Rather than doing the smart thing and getting out of the situation altogether, you stick around for a repeat of the abuse. Not only do you remain in the beating zone, you avail yourself of every opportunity to provoke the action. After all, you have been with this monster for a while and know exactly the right buttons to push, so why not push them? You've got something to say and that's all that matters. At the very least, you will end up in the emergency room and you have been there before, right? What difference do the black eyes, bruises, and cracked ribs make when the most important thing is that you got your verbal two cents in? Besides, this could be the one time that the beating doesn't stop until he kills you, and then all your problems with him will be over.

If you are one of these people, be honest with yourself. You are letting your emotions put you into situations that can get you hurt or killed. There are enough potential problems out there already; you don't need to hunt for them. Guys, learn to let the small things pass. The rest of the population does not wake up every morning with the sole mission of insulting you. It is quite likely that the rest of the population does not think of you at all. Most mistakes made by drivers are just that, mistakes. These errors come about as a result of too many other cars in close proximity to them, too many things on their mind other than driving, and not enough driving skill to begin with. Many times when something like this happens the person doesn't even realize that they did it. At any rate it's not worth a potential lethal encounter, is it? Being technically right in this situation will be of small comfort when you are nursing a gunshot wound.

Ladies, if you are in a violent domestic situation, get out of it, period. If violence has been part of the past it will be part of the future, I guarantee it. This guy is not going to change; if he has smacked you around before he will again. Whatever you do, don't egg the situation on. If you know what verbal buttons to push, try not pushing them. It doesn't mean that he is right and you are wrong, and it doesn't mean that you don't have a right to speak. It means not putting yourself deliberately into a set of circumstances that you know from painful experience to be dangerous.

The basic rule here is simple; there is plenty of trouble out there and if you go looking for it, you will probably be successful in your search.

Think! Don't hang around to be killed; retreat is an option.

If you find yourself in a bad situation, be it one that came to you or one that you dug up on your own, get out of it if you can. Retreat is an option, and you should try to exercise that option if the circumstances allow for it. Putting distance between yourself and trouble is a time-honored method of survival and it has been known to work quite well. Remember that as a private citizen you have no general obligation to stay in a fight.

Common sense dictates, however, that if you are going to exercise this option, you should first be sure that this option is available. In other words, if you are going to run away, make sure that you have a chance to get away and that you have somewhere to go to. Simply running may not be the answer and you could end up right back in the same situation that you attempted to flee from in the first place. It is a biological fact that the average man can outrun the average woman, so unfortunately, ladies, if you get into a foot race with a serial killer, he will probably cross the finish line first.

If running away is not an option, and unfortunately in a lot of cases it is not, then you will have to confront your attacker. My experience tells me that that is best done with some sort of weapon. When it comes to weapons, they all have their advantages and disadvantages.

The weapons in the arsenal: The most popular choice, chemical spray.

Pepper spray in all of its many different forms has been presented to the American public as the main alternative to owning a gun. Retailers sell these canisters by the millions across the country and they are touted far and wide as a viable substitute to owning a gun. If a rampaging felon confronts you, just give him a blast of this magic formula and he will quit what he is doing and immediately turn into a good citizen, no longer a threat to your safety. Women represent the primary customer base for this item and during the periodic times that there is a serial killer lurking about, you will be hard pressed to see a lady without one of these things dangling from her key chain. While there have certainly been some incidents in which this weapon was used effectively, it is my contention that totally relying on this chemical solution is a potentially deadly mistake.

The use of chemical agents is nothing new in the arena of human conflict and first came on the scene around four thousand years ago. As early as 2300 B.C. there were reported instances of Chinese soldiers dispersing enemy troops by burning red peppers in hot oil. These "stink pots" as they were called, produced an irritating and suffocating smoke and forced the enemy to seek somewhere else to stand. World War I saw the first massive use of chemical agents and, let loose amid the tightly packed troop formations on the western front, some of the results were horrific. After the war, there was an increasing interest in incorporating these agents into the law enforcement world. The theory was that these chemicals could be used to control uncooperative criminals and rioting mobs as effectively as they controlled enemy soldiers in wartime. The results have been mixed; nevertheless these devices have become standard issue for police officers in this country.

Pepper spray, or Chemical Mace as it used to be called, has been available to the general public for at least thirty-five years.

The formula has changed now and again but the anticipated use and intended results have always been the same. Most of these devices are designed to be sprayed into your attacker's face. The chemical agent causes an intense burning sensation to the eyes, nose, mouth, and any other damp tissue that it contacts. Additional effects include a tearing and swelling of the eyes, which can cause a decrease in vision. If the agent is inhaled, the resulting inflammation of the respiratory tract can temporarily restrict breathing to short shallow breaths.

In my opinion, there are some basic problems with the use of this implement as a primary defensive weapon. First of all, once the average buyer slaps down a credit card, he or she leaves the store thinking that all their self-protection problems are over. The canister is hung on the key chain, and the purchaser does no more. There is no practice session to determine how the implement works or how hard you have to press the trigger to get it to effectively disperse the chemical. I would go as far as to say that a large percentage of the women carrying these canisters for the protection of their very life have no idea of their effective range and whether the liquid comes out in a spray or a stream. If called upon to immediately activate their canister and hit a moving target in the face with the first blast, most of them would fail the test. The attacker would be on top of them before they could get the canister ready for firing.

The second problem with substituting a chemical agent for the ability to deliver deadly force is that you are doing just that, substituting. Getting hit with a chemical may cause someone to wish that they could die but it will not cause him to die. Human reaction to this compound is as varied as humans themselves. Some people are extremely sensitive and a dose of this medicine will shut them down but good. Other folks are, for one reason or another, resistant to the effects of these agents. Even if a particular person succumbs quickly to the initial exposure to one of these chemicals, if they are repeatedly exposed to the same mix, they will get used to it.

Ask your local cop and he will tell you about individual criminals becoming virtually immune to the effects of this weapon. Time and again a police encounter with a criminal has begun with the officer using chemical spray and finished with the officer using deadly force. They sprayed him and still ended up killing him, and this is the main thing that I want you to remember about the police use of this device. Yes, it is basic issue for an officer and they all wear it on their belts but keep in mind what else they wear on those belts. They are not called gun belts because they hold a can of chemical spray; they are called that because they hold a pistol. You will be very hard pressed to find a police officer that will venture onto the dark streets with just his can of liquid irritant and nothing else. Yes, they use it, but they use it knowing that they have other options, including deadly force.

If you plan on using this device for protection, then do yourself a favor and buy at least four canisters of the stuff. Use some of them to figure out the trigger mechanism and whatever safety device that it has. Observe the spray and see how far it will go. Practice hitting a face-sized target from various distances and positions, including flat on your back. Use as many canisters as necessary to become proficient and remember, your very life could depend on how well you manipulate this item. When you have mastered the device hang one on your key chain. Good luck.

The weapons in the arsenal: The martial arts myth.

Martial arts fighting techniques are another widely acclaimed method of self-defense. All across the country in times of an increased criminal threat, women are herded into self-defense classes and in the space of a few hours are turned into theoretical hand-to-hand combat experts. Men who have years of training and experience in this art usually teach these courses, and during the conduct of the training, the ladies are introduced to the magic of pain-inducing holds, grabs, kicks, and strikes. "If he comes at you, just do this," is the standard line given as the instructor tutors his student through the process of twisting and scratching. The presumption is that this short exposure will bring these women to the same level of proficiency that it took their instructors a decade or more to achieve. Of course, this training is conducted in a totally safe environment and is choreographed to provide good entertainment value. Fighting for your very life against a maniacal opponent will never be as precise and pretty as it is portrayed in one of these sessions. Just ask any street cop what it is really like and, he will tell a completely different story than "if he comes at you, just do this." Taking a combative suspect into custody usually requires the efforts of several officers and involves a lot of grunting, slugging, cursing, and gasping before things are under control. In some cases, the officer's entire defensive inventory is brought into play including pepper spray, batons, and the tender nibbles of a K-9 dog. It is only after the real fight is over that the opportunity arises to use all those wrist and thumb holds.

This is an area where the American public has been badly misled, primarily by the entertainment industry. I believe that their fictitious portrayal of martial arts as an effective weapon against criminal attack is at best misleading, and at worst dangerously deceptive. Movies and television dramas are chock full of characters punching, spinning, yelling, and kicking. In these scenarios, legions of bad guys are blithely knocked about and beaten into submission by the hero or heroine of the episode. The ranks of the defeated range all the way from common street thugs to international terrorists, and in some shows, even creators of the supernatural are beaten to a pulp for their sins. The truth is that the miscreants portrayed in these fantasy productions are far too cooperative and pain sensitive to be at all genuine. In the real world the outcome of the fight depends a lot on how the attacker reacts to your defensive moves. Just because you have hit him doesn't mean that he will just quit. More than likely you didn't hit him hard enough to change his mind about anything. In a hand-to-hand fight, size and strength matter and they matter a whole bunch. That is just the way it is. If a 100-pound karate master squares off against a 300-pound drunk lumberjack, he will probably lose. In order to be effective, a kick or punch has to have force behind it, and the amount of force is largely dependent on the body weight and strength of the person who throws it. It is a simple matter of physics.

Defensive techniques such as these require years of intensive practice on the part of the individual if they are going to be at all effective. Even then you had better hope that your opponent is in a cooperative frame of mind. Even if you have been practicing and are becoming proficient in one technique or another, there is no telling what the outcome is going to be. If you are like most people and have only taken a few sessions (because there is a serial killer on the loose and you're scared) then you have probable wasted your time and money. If you are not going to make a real commitment to learning this art then you should forget it.

The weapons in the arsenal: The good old ball bat.

Of all the methods of self-defense that people tote around in lieu of a firearm I think the one that I find the most uninspiring is the baseball bat. When I see a woman, who maybe weighs ninety-five pounds dripping wet, sporting a Louisville Slugger and claiming that they will just whack their opponent into submission, I just have to turn away and shake my head. Yeah, ladies, if you are lucky enough to catch your prospective murderer while he is passed out drunk and you have a half hour or so to work on him, a ball bat is just the thing. You could take your time orbiting the bed, slamming and thumping wherever you think necessary. Maybe, just maybe, he will cooperate and lie still for your attentions and if you hit all the right places enough times, he might not wake up, take the bat away from you, and reverse the process.

A serial killer is probably not going to so kind as to give you warning and align himself with the business end of your bat. Your first clue that he is there is more than likely going to be when he is crawling through your window in the wee hours. Try swinging a ball bat in a hallway that is three and a half feet wide sometime and see how many times you can hit your target effectively. I've got news for you ladies; men themselves are not particularly afraid of another guy sporting a bat and will usually not run away from a confrontation like that. As I told you before, the moderately conditioned male body can take an unbelievable impact and keep right on coming. Again ask your local street cop about this and have him recount the number of times that he has knocked some guy into next week only to have the miscreant get up and continue the war. I'm not saying for a minute that if you round house some guy with a two handed swing that it's not going to hurt. It will hurt like no tomorrow, but that is no guarantee that he will change his plans in the face of excruciating pain.

What you are really doing with a ball bat is trying to fight a twenty-first century battle using a club, a weapon as old as mankind. Trying to crush each other's skulls is what the cave men used to do, and they eventually found a different way. My advice is to put the bat away and save it for the after-work games.

The weapons in the arsenal: "Equal or greater force" The practical side of owning a gun for protection.

With all the choices for defense against a vicious criminal attack, why choose a gun? Why select a defensive tool that carries with it a tremendous amount of responsibility and some potential hazard? Isn't life complicated enough keeping up with the daily grind without adding a lethal weapon to the list? The answer to that question is quite simple. Unlike all the other options that we have talked about, a firearm allows you to confront you attacker with equal or greater

Equal Or Greater Force

force. With the introduction of this implement into the fight, the playing field levels considerably. If your opponent has his own gun, you now stand equal to him. If he is so foolish as to come to your murder without a gun, then you now have the capability to bring more force to bear against him than he can bring against you. If you are mentally prepared to use that weapon, you now have the upper hand in the situation.

A firearm is designed to inflict a lethal injury on a human being and, if used correctly, that is exactly what it will do. Suddenly it's not so important how big or threatening your attacker is, you can cut him down to size in a hurry. Does your attacker imagine himself to be cold and unfeeling, unconcerned with the pain and suffering he brings to others? Well, that pistol in your hand is a thousand time more cold and unfeeling than a human murderer could ever be. If you shoot him with it, he will be hurt and hurt bad; in fact, there is a reasonable chance that he will die. That is what a firearm brings to the table, the capability to deliver lethal force against your attacker. That's the good news; now for the bad news.

Because a firearm can be used to deliver lethal force, owning one puts you into a position of great responsibility and potential liability. So, do yourself a big favor and conduct a little research before you take this step. Most impulse purchases that you make will bring you little harm other than the damage done to your checking account. On the other hand, owning a gun brings with it some enormous obligations. These responsibilities break down into two main areas, use and storage.

If you look around your home, you will discover that many potential hazards exist. If you are smart you have recognized these potential troubles and have taken some steps to deal with them. Having children around makes these precautions absolutely necessary, and this is doubly true when it comes to firearms. Proper storage of a gun means that you have to find a logical balance between safety and availability. Obviously, you will want to store your weapon in a place where the wrong person cannot pick it up. On the other hand,

The weapons in the arsenal

the weapon will do you no good if it is not available when you need it. Locking up your gun at one end of the house and the ammunition at the other will greatly decrease the potential for accident, but it will make things difficult when the time comes to use the weapon. The choices are many and they all have some advantages and disadvantages. Trigger locks are good but they do not conceal the weapon from prying eyes or curious fingers. A small safe of some sort is good as long as you can get into it when you need to. Your best course of action is to visit your local gun store and have them advise you on your options for storage.

Your second main responsibility when it comes to owning a gun for self-defense is to be proficient in its use. The only way to do that is to get some training. In order to be proficient with a firearm, you must be able to load it, unload it, clear a stoppage, and hit your target when the time comes. This is probably not something that you can figure out on your own, so go get some professional instruction and when you do, be careful because there can be some pitfalls.

One of the biggest problems that you can run into when you go to get some firearms instruction is the male ego. This is true whether you are male or female, but it really comes to the surface when the instruction is being presented to women. For some reason, every guy that has ever looked at a gun thinks that he is some sort of expert in their use. This is bad enough, but at the same time he also imagines that he is some sort of expert when it comes to instructing others in their use. Even if he has had some training in firearms proficiency, he usually has had no training on how to teach firearms proficiently. I have been a professional firearms and tactics instructor for many years now and I continually run into this problem. The problem is compounded when these individuals are set loose to train inexperienced women in this craft. In this set of circumstances, the ego of the instructor can make the training ineffective and sometimes dangerous.

Instructing people in the use of weapons is just as much of a skill as the ability to use the weapon itself. When you go forth to seek instruction, shop around a bit. Simple ability with a weapon does not, in and of itself, make for a good instructor. I have known plenty of people whose skill with a firearm has to be seen to be believed yet at the same time they are very poor instructors. You will know a good instructor by his demeanor, patience, willingness to listen, and lack of bragging about his own abilities. A good firearms instructor will not belittle or make fun of the fact that you are nervous about learning to shoot. He will instead calmly walk you and talk you through the process. When he demonstrates the manipulation of the weapon, he will do it slowly enough for you to see what he is doing and not use that situation as an opportunity to show off.

Owning a gun for protection is something that you need to think about before you make the move. In order to avoid potential pitfalls, you must seek out those around you who are familiar with this option. Listen to what they have to say and make your decision after you have pondered the subject a while. A deadly weapon should never be an impulse purchase. If you do choose to employ this method of defense, know that you will be choosing sides in an ongoing argument.

Firearms, truth vs. propaganda

Private ownership and use of firearms is one of the more controversial subjects that our society faces today. Any mention of this issue is guaranteed to result in some sort of verbal confrontation between the two sides. There seems to be no middle ground or room for compromise. The media demonizes them, Hollywood glorifies them, and the sheer number of falsehoods that are put forth on the subject of guns is enough to boggle the mind.

More years ago than I like to think about, I was a young U.S. Army sergeant attending the Special Forces qualification course at Fort Bragg, North Carolina. The particular specialty that I had chosen

The weapons in the arsenal

to qualify in was heavy and light weapons. The course consisted of many weeks of intensive training in just about all the military weapons in use throughout the world today. Late one evening I found myself listening to a national news commentary as I studied for a test. All around me on tables, chairs, and countertops were literally dozens of Army weapons manuals. As I pored through these guidebooks, I had half an ear on the conversation taking place on the news show. After a while I realized that the subject being discussed was firearms and the ability of the average citizen to possess one. The guest being interviewed was obviously against the concept of gun ownership among the general populace and was seeking to make his point by concentrating on the issue of safety.

"They just can't be trusted" he said, "they could go off at any time." "You mean they just go off without any reason?" the commentator asked. "That's right," was the reply, "one minute they are just sitting there, and the next thing you know they just fire."

Now at this point it was clear that the commentator was somewhat incredulous, despite the fact that he was on the side of the one being interviewed. "I find that a little hard to swallow" was his next comment. "I'm telling you, guns will just go off for no reason, and those are the facts," replied the guest. Momentarily stunned, I began looking through the many manuals spread around the kitchen and living room. Had I missed something? Nowhere in the last several weeks had the concept of a self-actuating firearm been discussed in the weapons course. Everything else had been covered in detail, but no mention of a gun that would fire on its own volition. I could find no mention of it in the manuals either. Something was definitely wrong here. An intriguing concept if it existed. Still, the news show guest had not made it clear if the weapon he spoke of would fire only when it decided to or could be made to fire on command, and that would certainly be important.

Obviously, the individual being interviewed had no idea of what he was talking about. There is no such thing as guns that will simple decide to shoot and then carry that decision out. They simply don't exist. What was disturbing about the interview was that his words were not really challenged beyond a single doubting sentence uttered by the commentator. That bothered me so I began to keep track of the subject in an impromptu investigation of my own. For the next six months I made an effort to watch my television anytime the subject of firearms was brought up, whether in the news or some other program and to do the same thing while reading. At the end of my study, I had heard the subject mentioned approximately one hundred times. This was a combination of both television and news magazine articles dealing with the issue in one form or another. Of the one hundred references to the subject, there were only three that did not contain information that I knew to be completely false. I am not talking about slanting or editorializing the issue; I am talking about outright falsehoods being put forth as fact to an unwitting public. Now if someone were to take the witness stand in a court case, and make ninety-three false statements to the jury, he would find himself on trial for perjury and would face a stiff sentence if convicted. Remember that the next time you hear those in the news media chattering about guns in the hands of private citizens. Do yourself a favor and conduct a little private research on the statements that they make. You will be surprised at what you discover. Most of the coverage on the subject of citizens owning guns is nothing more than pure propaganda.

In the presentation of that propaganda, the main case that is made against the private ownership of firearms is that they theoretically represent a danger to the public at large. The hypothesis is that the weapons themselves are dangerous and therefore automatically present a danger to anyone in the general vicinity of them. Because they are dangerous, the reasoning goes, the average citizen should be prohibited from owning or possessing one. In most cases, the subject gets probed no deeper than that. As with a lot of things, the truth is a bit more complex.

The fact is that there are all sorts of dangers involved with living on Planet Earth. Mother Nature creates some, and your fellow human beings concoct others. Some are obvious and some not so obvious.

The weapons in the arsenal

Some dangers you can do something about and some you cannot. Some dangers are inherent and some only have potential. The main difference between the two is the amount of human interaction that is required for the object or situation to be dangerous.

An on-coming hurricane or exploding volcano is inherently dangerous because our actions or lack thereof have no effect on those objects. They will bring harm and there is no human decision that will stop them, short of getting out of their way. A debilitating or deadly disease that has no known cure falls into the same category. Life on Planet Earth is full of these threats and there is little that you can do about most of them. Even if you dodge the main hazards associated with human existence, the simple passage of time will eventually do you in.

Most manmade objects fall into the category of a potential threat. Unlike the hurricane, volcano, or rampaging virus, a manmade object requires the action of a human being in order to be dangerous. In your daily life you are surrounded by these potential threats. From the other drivers on the road each day to the quality of construction in the building that you work in, you are continually at risk due to the actions or inactions of the people around you. However, since that set of circumstances is not preordained or inevitable, there is only potential harm in these objects or circumstances. Firearms fall into this same category and, therefore, it is my contention they are only potentially harmful, not inherently so.

A gun, be it a pistol, rifle, or shotgun, is designed to propel a projectile/s out of its barrel and send it/them flying a certain distance. It is used to inflict damage or injury as a result of that projectile striking something or someone. In order for the weapon to do that, it has to be picked up and made to do that. A human being has to pick up the weapon and use it or it will do nothing.

One of the most important issues that are deliberately overlooked in any discourse by those who are against firearm ownership is the fact that while guns are certainly potentially dangerous, they are also potentially helpful. Each day in the United States there are multiple incidents wherein guns are used for legitimate self-protection. In these cases, the presence of that weapon serves a good purpose in the same way that a weapon used in the commission of a crime serves a bad purpose. In any society one of the most dangerous potential hazards that you face is the ill will and intent of another human being. Used properly, a firearm can counter and eliminate that danger.

In some of the most blatant examples of hypocrisy in our society today, individuals in positions of authority or popularity scoff at the idea of regular citizens owning guns, all the while living under the protection of armed security personnel. In other words, they are anti-gun and, at the same time, people with guns protect their lives. Safe and secure behind the protection offered by a weapon, they actively seek to deny others that same security. They never met you personally and probably never will, yet they unhesitatingly maintain that you are not to be trusted to possess the same level of protection for your life that they are for theirs. They have deemed you, the average citizen, to be untrustworthy and incompetent, and you didn't get to utter a single word on your own behalf. What a deal.

When you hear one of these people rattle on about the evils of gun ownership and how they should not be allowed into the hands of the average citizen, remember one important fact. Should you find yourself in the unfortunate position of being directly confronted by a person with murderous intent, none of these people will be there to help you out. You will not be able to call Hillary Clinton or Dianne Feinstein for assistance. Oprah Winfrey will not come running as the serial killer creeps toward you, and Sharon Stone will not throw herself between you and him. No, you will be on your own in that encounter, and you will either survive or you will not. If you fail to live through this horrific situation, further understand that none of the crusaders against guns will be showing up at your funeral. Michael Moore will not stand weeping as they shovel dirt over you, and Sarah Brady will not be there to console those that you left behind. If that unfortunate event ever occurs, all of those good folks will go about their lives, unknowing and unconcerned about your fate, protected by people with guns.

I solidly support the right of the individual citizen to own a firearm. For me, however, the issue goes much deeper than safety or protection although that is certainly part of it. In my opinion, the private ownership of weapons symbolizes a populace that is unwilling to surrender all control to the government. That is a good thing, as governments have shown us throughout history that they are not to be trusted with total control over the lives of their citizens. When the average citizen takes direct responsibility for his or her own protection, they are making a statement to the controlling authority. They are telling that authority that they can take care of themselves and do not need to be cared for and this, my friends, is the very foundation of a free society. We cannot claim to live in freedom unless we, as individuals, are willing to shoulder the main responsibilities in our lives. I further contend that one of those main responsibilities in your life is the protection of that life.

Edged weapons, nasty but effective

If you choose not to own a gun, yet still seek an effective implement for self-defense, there is an alternative available. Be warned, though, that this choice is not for the squeamish and I would maintain that to use it effectively requires the same level of commitment that a firearm does. Used effectively, an edged weapon can cause tremendous injury in a short time and, like any other weapon, it has advantages and disadvantages. The main disadvantage of an edged weapon is that it is not a gun and, therefore, you must make physical contact with your attacker in order to use it. The main advantage of an edged weapon is that it is not a gun and, therefore, does not carry with it the legal and safety concerns that a firearm does.

When it comes to carrying an edged weapon for self-defense, the single best choice is the ordinary box knife. It is inexpensive, sturdy, easy to use, and hellishly effective. It can be employed effectively

Equal Or Greater Force

using natural defensive hand and arm motions. Using your hand to swat at someone when they reach for you is a natural body movement that you can do without having to think about it. Put a razorblade in that same hand and the effects are amazing. If you attacker does manage to grab you, start cutting, and you will definitely get their attention. In a few seconds you will have critically wounded your attacker, and he will probably be rethinking his plant to murder you. Not for the faint-hearted but effective.

Whatever your choice of weapon for self defense, make sure that you know how to use it and under what circumstances you can use it legally. Remember, with the fresh air of freedom comes the mantle of responsibility.

Chapter 7
The Aftermath

"A court is a place where what was confused before becomes more unsettled than ever."

Henry Waldorf Francis

"Facts are facts and will not disappear on account of your likes."

Jawaharlal Nehru

The way you handle yourself after a lethal force confrontation is just as important as the way you handle things during the actual confrontation. At this point, the physical danger is gone, but you are by no means out of the woods when it comes to potential harm to your life, as you know it. You are now in a situation where words are just as important as actions, and both your words and your actions can get you in some real hot water. We do not live in a society where you can use deadly force on another human being and simply walk away after it is finished. Killing or seriously injuring someone, even in a clear-cut act of self-defense, is guaranteed to get the attention of your local law enforcement organization. That organization is going to conduct an investigation of the incident and will arrive at certain conclusions based on their observations and experience. Regardless of the circumstances of your confrontation, there is absolutely no guarantee that the persons investigating the incident will reach a conclusion that is in your favor. Recognize this possibility beforehand and be ready to deal with it.

Accept the fact that there is a difference between fairness and justice.

Most of us were raised to believe in a concept called fairness, a system of balanced results, so to speak. Most of us were also raised to believe in the concept of justice and in fact, most of us walk around thinking that the two are one and the same. The truth of the matter is that sometimes they are the same and sometimes they are not.

Webster's Dictionary's description of "fair" takes up a quarter of a page as it meanders through all of the possible meanings for this word. The most pertinent description that I was able to dig out goes like this: "fair implies the treating of all sides alike, justly and equitably." According to this belief, if someone attempts to do something bad to you and something bad happens to him or her in the process, then that is okay. In other words, if an individual attempts to murder you and, instead, you take his life, then that is only fair, isn't it? And, if that is true, why should you suffer in the aftermath at the hands of the legal system? After all, the dictionary description of what fairness means even contains a reference to justice, doesn't it?

When we look up "justice" in the dictionary, we come up with a little shorter and more concise description of its meaning than we did with "fair." The description of justice goes like this: "the quality of conforming to principles of reason, to generally accepted standards of right and wrong, and to the stated terms of laws, rules, agreements, etc., in matters affecting persons who could be wronged or unduly favored." Certainly there are some similarities between the two concepts, but there is a difference also. In the aftermath of a self-defense killing, you need to be aware of this difference and how that could affect you.

Justice is based upon the law, and fairness is based on individual perception. Another way of saying it is that fairness is an outlook or attitude, and justice is a consequence. At first glance they would

The Aftermath

seem to be the same. After all, fairness is justice, isn't it? What is deemed to be fair must also fall within the realm of what is just, should it not? In some instances this holds true, since there have been situations wherein the legal result of a situation fell within the bounds of what the average person would consider to be fair. Situations have also come to pass wherein what was considered fair also fell within the letter of the law. Yet there is still no guarantee that this will happen in your particular case.

There have been, and will continue to be, situations where the concept of justice did not square with the perception of fairness. We have all heard of instances where average citizens defended themselves with lethal force and survived, only to be ground up by the legal system. Sometimes these situations resulted in the person's facing civil action, i.e., a lawsuit. Sometimes the circumstances were much more grim and the hapless citizen ended up in front of a jury facing criminal charges. When this happens, everyone around is outraged because after all, "they were just defending themselves and don't we have a right to do that?"

The thing to remember is this: the law is the law and not your buddy. The system of laws that we live under was not put in place to make sure that you never have any bad experiences with them. They were not even put there to make sure that everything is fair, as that would be an impossible task. The laws that we live under are there to ensure that our society functions as smoothly as possible, period.

The law of the land

If you are going to be subject to the law of the land governing this issue, then it is certainly prudent to find out a little about the wording and meaning of that law. While the homicide statutes are somewhat similar across the nation, there are also some subtle differences as you go from state to state. I happen to live in Louisiana so I will use that state's statute as my primary example. If you don't live in Louisiana, it would behoove you to find out the exact wording and meaning of the law in your own state.

Louisiana Revised Statute 14:20 pertains to justifiable homicide. If you find yourself in a position where you had to use deadly force on another human being, your legal standing will be determine based on this statute. This ordinance is broken down into four separate paragraphs for easier understanding. I will go over each one and its intended meaning in an attempt to give a layman's explanation. Before I do, however, I will make the following plain statement and would ask you to keep that statement in mind as you read further. I am not now, nor do I ever plan to be, a lawyer of any type. I have nothing against the profession, it just doesn't interest me. Therefore, if you have any doubts or questions about this statute or just want more information on the meaning of these paragraphs, see an attorney. I state right here and now that I will automatically defer to anything that they have to say on the subject that may differ with my explanation.

Louisiana Statute 14:20

Paragraph 1 of the statute states that:

A homicide is justifiable:

(1) When committed in self-defense by one who reasonably believes that he is in imminent danger of losing his life or receiving great bodily harm and that the killing is necessary to save himself from that danger.

The key words in this statement are "reasonable belief," and those words are repeated throughout the statute. In other words, at the moment in question you were in genuine fear for your life or in

The Aftermath

fear of great bodily injury. It can be discovered later that no such threat actually existed at that moment and you can still be found justified in your actions by the legal system. It is all about your perception at the actual moment and whether your actions of that moment seem reasonable based on that perception.

Paragraph 2 of the statute states that:

A homicide is justifiable:

(2) When committed for the purpose of preventing a violent or forcible felony involving danger to life or great bodily harm by one who reasonably believes that such an offense is about to be committed and that such action is necessary for its prevention. The circumstances must be sufficient to excite the fear of a reasonable person that there would be serious danger to his own life or person if he attempted to prevent the felony without the killing.

This paragraph is referring to a situation where the moment has not actually occurred but the prospective victim has a reasonable belief that it will occur in the near future. The situation must be one in which the person is in fear for his or her life and believes that the only way to be saved from becoming a victim of great harm is to use deadly force to prevent that harm.

Paragraph 3 of the statute states that:

A homicide is justifiable:

(3) When committed against a person whom one reasonably

> believes to be likely to use any unlawful force against a person present in a dwelling or place of business, or when committed against a person whom one reasonably believes is attempting to use any unlawful force against a person present in a motor vehicle as defined in R.S. 32:1 (40), while committing or attempting to commit a burglary or robbery of such dwelling, business, or motor vehicle. The homicide shall be justifiable even though the person does not retreat from the encounter.

This paragraph is focused toward an encounter in a home, business, or other structure. Those structures include a person's automobile, which, under Louisiana law, is considered to be an extension of one's home. The key point in this paragraph is that the intended victim has no obligation to retreat from the encounter as long as he is occupying one of those structures. If you don't live in Louisiana, you had better go check and see what your state statute has to say on this matter. Some states are similar in outlook and believe a person's home and other such structures to be his or her castle, so to speak. Other supposedly enlightened and progressive states actually demand that a person run away from their own home during such an incident. Those same states stand fully ready to prosecute any individual who did not give ground to the criminal in this situation. Fortunately, I don't have to live in one of those states. If I did, I don't think that I could go through my day thinking that my home was actually mine. Instead, I would have to consider it nothing more than a temporary dwelling that was open to invasion by anyone who saw fit to invade it, but that's just me.

Paragraph 4 of the statute states that:

A homicide is justifiable:

(4) When committed by a person lawfully inside a dwelling, a place of business, or a motor vehicle as defined in R.S. 32:1 (40), against a person who is attempting to make an unlawful entry into the dwelling, place of business, or motor vehicle, or who has made an unlawful entry into the dwelling, place of business, or motor vehicle and the person committing the homicide reasonably believes that the use of deadly force is necessary to prevent the entry or to compel the intruder to leave the premises or motor vehicle. The homicide shall be justifiable even though the person committing the homicide does not retreat from the encounter.

This paragraph puts some real teeth in paragraph 3 as it maintains that you have a right to prevent the intrusion into the said structure before it actually occurs. This section was added to the Louisiana statute in 1997 and became known as the "shoot the burglar law." The addition of this paragraph into the statute caused a nationwide controversy as people lined up on either side of the issue. Detractors maintained that the result would be a virtual green light to prospective vigilantes lurking in Louisiana society. To prove their case, they pointed to an unfortunate occurrence that had taken place in a small town outside of Baton Rouge in 1992. In this incident, a Japanese exchange student was shot and killed in a carport by a Louisiana citizen who had mistaken his intentions. The reality is that the fourth paragraph of this law was not even on the books at the time of this incident and, therefore, did not apply. In fact, the circumstances of the incident itself were not totally relevant to this part of the law. While it does raise some legitimate concerns about the perception of an individual confronting a criminal in these circumstances, the wording of the paragraph is quite clear, at least to me. In this situation you have to have a reasonable belief that if you don't prevent the ongoing intrusion, you will suffer grave harm as a result.

Louisiana Statute 14:22, which accompanies **Louisiana Statute 14:20**, covers the subject of the defense of people other than yourself. While this situation doesn't happen as often as a direct encounter with a criminal, it is still in the realm of possibility and therefore important to know.

Louisiana Statute 14:22 states:

It is justifiable to use force or violence or to kill in the defense of another person when it is reasonably apparent that the person attacked could have justifiably used such means himself, and when it is reasonably believed that such intervention is necessary to protect the other person.

This statute tells you that you can use lethal force to defend others if necessary. The qualifier is still based on reasonable belief. In this case it has to be apparent that the victim himself is justified to use that level of force if he were able.

All of the statutes governing the use of lethal force are based on the concept of reasonable belief on the part of the potential victim. A reasonable belief is best described as a belief that would appear reasonable under the recounted circumstances to an ordinary and prudent person. To be deemed justified in your actions, you have to be able to convince others that, were they faced with the same set of circumstances, they would have reacted in a similar manner. It is all based on the perception of the moment, the feelings of the moment, and your ability to recount that moment.

The role of law enforcement

If you ever find yourself going through this unfortunate process, you are going to deal directly with the representatives of law enforcement. I am fairly certain that I know what you will be thinking as the police question you and you watch them go about their investigation. You will be wondering, maybe silently and maybe aloud, where all the concern for life and death was when you were getting ready to lose your life. You will look at the officers around you and wonder where they were when you were trying your best not to get murdered. They surely seemed to get there quickly when it was time to come and decide if what you did was right or wrong; but they were nowhere around when you had to do it, were they? I certainly understand this sentiment, but I need to point out a few realities.

The police officers who respond to a situation such as this are not there to judge you or what you did. Certainly they have personal opinions and, if it is clearly a case of self-defense, they are probably more sympathetic to your circumstances than you might believe. Still, they have a job to do and that job is to conduct an investigation of the incident. As to where they were when you were busy trying to stay alive, well, they were not there and that's it. As I explained in Chapter four, the police are few and far between, and they cannot be everywhere at once. They got to your scene so quickly because you or someone else called them and told them to come. Giving them the evil eye and asking them in a sarcastic tone where they were may feel good to say, but it is immaterial to the situation. This is a time when you want to keep your emotions under control to the greatest extent possible. While no two incidents of this type are alike, and the outcome is unknown, there are some general rules to follow. I collected all of the information contained in the rest of this chapter during consultations with currently serving homicide investigators, and practicing attorneys, so read carefully.

Equal Or Greater Force

The first person that you will have to contend with in the aftermath of a lethal use of force situation is the homicide investigator assigned to the case. He or she is not there to decide if you were right or wrong in your actions. Others will do that, if it gets that far. This is the individual who is charged with finding out what happened, documenting what happened, and making further recommendations as to what should happen next.

When the investigator arrives on the scene and begins to question you, one of the first things that he is trying to determine is how you arrived at the decision to do whatever it was that you did. What led you to the use of lethal force? What was your reasonable belief? He will use several things to accomplish this task, including a consultation with whoever the first responder to the incident was. More than likely this will be the uniformed patrol officer who was first on the scene and therefore the first person with a badge to talk to you. When you talk to this officer, keep in mind that he or she has been trained to remember exactly what you say and how you say it so that they can pass that information on to the investigator later. As much as humanly possible, this officer will recount your exact words and demeanor. Upon receiving this information, the homicide investigator will probably question you himself to see if your story has changed any from the time that you originally recounted it to the first responding officer. If your statement has not changed in any significant way, then that tells the investigator that you are confident in what you did and that counts for you. If it has changed, that indicates a lack of confidence in your decision and he will begin to look harder at the situation. Here is one of major pitfalls that you can encounter.

When you tell the police what happened do just that, tell them what happened and only what happened. Be truthful but don't second-guess yourself, don't wonder if you could have done it any differently, and, above all, don't embellish. Keep it simple and just recount the facts, as you know them. If something is unclear, say so. Don't search around for an answer that may not be there. In the aftermath of this type of situation, your memory of the event may not be clear for several days. If you don't remember something, say so and leave it at that. Don't unnecessarily run your mouth and get yourself in trouble. The homicide investigator is not there to determine whether you were right or wrong, since that job belongs to others. Don't try to convince him that you were right. Just tell him what happened.

The investigator will be trying to determine whether what you say is credible or not. If the physical evidence at the scene can back up what you are telling him, then your story will lean toward the credible side. If the evidence conflicts with your statement, then he will continue to dig. As he conducts his investigation of the scene, the investigator will entertain the notion that the person you killed may be the actual victim in the situation. This may cause you some outrage but it is part of his job, and any conflicts between your story and the physical evidence at the scene will cause him to look harder in this direction. Whatever you do, never try to stage the scene prior to the arrival of the police. We have all heard someone say that if they have to shoot someone that they will just put a knife in their hand and drag them inside. That may have worked one hundred years ago, but it will not work now. Modern technology has caught up with crime scene investigation with a vengeance and, if you did this, it will be obvious sooner or later. You are physically incapable of deceiving this technology, so let the body lie where it fell and don't try to improve your case. If it is discovered that you did try to stage the scene for your own benefit, you will then become the main subject of the investigation and things will become decidedly more unpleasant than they already are.

If you decide to say nothing to the police, that is your constitutional right and it cannot be taken from you. It will, however, cause the police to look harder at the situation and you. If the facts are on your side it will not matter in the long run, so if you take this route stick with it. If you call an attorney that is the advice that he or she will probably give you anyway. The investigator may actually be sympathetic to your circumstances but he will not tell you that and, in any event, he is not there as a friend.

The relationship, if any, between the shooter and the person shot will have a direct impact on the level to which that case is investigated. If you are a single mother with two small children in the house and the person that you killed was a total stranger who forced his way into you home against your will, then the initial investigation will be conducted fairly quickly. However, if the person that you killed was your ex-husband or current boyfriend, then it's going to take a little longer and be more complicated. If it was a situation of husband vs. wife or boyfriend vs. girlfriend, then the investigator will examine the possibility that you in some way contributed to the situation. He will examine the history of the relationship and the circumstances that brought you two face to face. The investigator has to keep this possibility in mind because it is a possibility. Any domestic situation will come under far more scrutiny that a case of stranger vs. stranger.

Like it or not, gender and physical stature will also play a role in the investigation. If you are a two hundred pound male who lifts weights for entertainment, then you are going to get looked at harder than the one hundred pound single mother. If the act was justified, it will make no difference in the long run, but it will definitely be a factor in the questioning. Whatever the circumstances, keep your emotions under control, especially if you are male.

The role of the lawyers

Once the initial procedures at the actual scene are completed, the investigation will pass on to the lawyers. The attorneys involved will originate from two different sides of the issue, those who prosecute and those who defend, and they can both have a major impact on your life. The degree to which these people become involved in the matter will be totally determined by the circumstances of the incident. If the situation appears to be a cut and dried case of self-defense, then the prosecutor may decline to pursue the matter and it

The Aftermath

will be over. If the circumstances are a little vague, or it is a high-profile case, then the prosecutor may pursue the matter further. The next step will be for him to present the case to a grand jury and it is their job to decide if the case actually goes to trial.

When the grand jury convenes, only they and the prosecuting attorney are present. If you have retained the services of a defense lawyer, then he may be allowed to present a statement on your behalf, but basically he is out of the game at this point. This may sound unfair but it is really not and, in any event, that is the way the process works. If the grand jury decides not to indict you and send you to trial then, again, the situation ends right there. If the opposite happens and you are bound over for trial, then the situation will drag on for some time and life will change. At that point you will be arrested and charged with a crime.

Defense lawyers have become the subject of a lot of contempt and derision in our society, and it can be argued that some of those opinions may be justified. Like them or not, however, you will view them entirely differently on the day that you need the services of one. In that set of circumstances, your lawyer may well be the only friend that you have, so do as instructed. If he tells you to keep your mouth shut, then keep it shut and don't argue with him. This attorney has forgotten more about the law than you will ever know so let him handle things. You are paying him to do a job on your behalf, so let him do it. Even if he comes up with a defense strategy that initially makes no sense to you, go along with it. Always keep in mind the fact that your lawyer knows things about the process that you don't.

One of the things that was emphasized by the lawyers that I talked to was the fact that the statement "everything you say can and will be used against you" has some real legal teeth. You can have a completely confidential conversation with only four types of people in this world: your lawyer, a doctor, a member of the clergy, or your spouse. Anything that you say to anyone else about the incident can be legally discovered and brought into the trial process. That brings us right back to the "keep your mouth shut" syndrome. You cannot get into trouble for a statement that you never make; the opposite is most definitely not true. Don't speak of regrets or self-doubts to any one but your lawyer and, above all, don't brag to anyone about killing someone to anyone, ever.

Whatever happens, be glad that you are alive and are around for the aftermath.

Surviving a murderous attack on your person only to be ground up in the legal system is something that is terrible to contemplate and even more terrible to endure. To have your life torn apart, right after you came so close to losing it, is something that I hope you never have to go through. If you do go through this ordeal, then I want you to keep a few things in mind.

Bad things happen to all of us and when they do, it is natural to think that your life has ended. It seems at the moment that this thing will never end and all is lost. Bad things do end, though, and so will this. However long you ordeal lasts, it will not last forever. "Nothing good or bad lasts forever," the saying goes, and it is true. Even if the worst happens and you find yourself behind bars for a while, that too will come to a close. There will come a day when you look around you and realize that it is finally over.

During your ordeal and forever after, remember this: you are still alive and that beats the alternative. The alternative in this situation was to have been killed and that is a set of circumstances that will last forever. Remember, the legal system is temporary, but the graveyard is permanent.

Epilogue

"Courage is not just one of the virtues but the form of every virtue at the testing point."

C.S. Lewis

I sincerely hope that you and your loved ones are never in a position in which you need the advice contained in this book. It is my wish that you live out your days in peace and security and are never confronted with a violent attack on your person. Having made that wish, I know that it is an unrealistic one at best. Like it or not, the threat of violence surrounds us, and it will happen to some of you no matter what I wish for.

If it does happen, stay strong, stay brave, and do your utmost to come out the other end of the ordeal still alive. Those who love you and depend on you have a right for you to be around. You have a responsibility to them to survive if you can.

If this unfortunate event befalls you after reading this book, then it is my further hope that the memories of my words help you come through the situation and deal with the aftermath. Good luck and God Bless America and you.

Kit Cessna

Baton Rouge, 2004

About the Author

Kit Cessna served in the 1st Special Forces Operational Detachment-Delta (Delta Force), 2nd Ranger Battalion and the 1st Special Forces Group as an A-Team member. While in Delta Force, he saw combat action in the 1989 invasion of Panama. He traveled to over 50 different countries during his military career before retiring in 1994. Currently, he is an instructor for the U.S. State Department Anti-Terrorism Assistance Program (ATAP) and is the lead instructor for the Southern Anti-Terrorist Regional Training Academy (SARTA) in Louisiana. He has served as a reserve SWAT officer for two police departments. He is married with two children and resides in Baton Rouge.

Printed in the United States
27028LVS00002B/51